TO

DATE			

Other Books by John Rosemond

John Rosemond's Six-Point Plan for Raising Happy, Healthy Children

Ending the Homework Hassle: Understanding, Preventing, and Solving School Performance Problems

Parent Power! A Common-Sense Approach to Parenting in the '90s and Beyond

Making the "Terrible" Twos Terrific!

TO SPANK OR NOT TO SPANK

A PARENTS' HANDBOOK

John K. Rosemond

Illustrated by Jeff Koterba

Foreword by
Richard Wexler, Author of *Wounded Innocents*

Andrews and McMeel
A Universal Press Syndicate Company
Kansas City

Designed by Barrie Maguire.

Library of Congress Cataloging-in-Publication Data

Rosemond, John K., 1947–
    To spank or not to spank: a parents' handbook / John K.
Rosemond ; illustrated by Jeff Koterba ; foreword by Richard Wexler.
        p.   cm.
    Includes bibliographical references.
    ISBN 0-8362-2813-8
    1. Corporal punishment. 2. Discipline of children. 3. Child
rearing. I. Title.
HQ770.4.R67   1994
649'.64—dc20   94-30050
                                                                    CIP

To my mother, Emily;

my father, Jack;

and my stepfather, Julius

CONTENTS

Experience should teach us to be most on our guard to protect liberty when the Government's purposes are benificent. Men born to freedom are naturally alert to repel invasion of their liberty by evil-minded rulers. The greatest dangers to liberty lurk in insidious encroachment by men of zeal, well-meaning but without understanding.

—Supreme Court Justice
Louis D. Brandeis, 1856–1941

ACKNOWLEDGMENTS

It takes only one person to come up with an idea for a book, but it takes many people to make it happen. In this case, the book you're holding in your hands would have been a piece of tedious, overwrought trash (you may think it is anyway) if not for the support, encouragement, and advice I received from the following individuals:

• Robert Larzelere, a fine psychologist and a fine researcher, who was more than generous with his work, his time, and his most helpful suggestions. Thanks for your willingness to stick yourself out on a limb, Bob.

• Richard Wexler—author, professor, and fellow iconoclast—one of those rare individuals who has the courage to point out when the emperor is wearing no clothes, the passion to write an entire book about the emperor's nudity, and the skill to write an excellent one at that! Thanks for the great foreword.

• Reed Bell, M.D., who came along at just the right time in the writing of this book with just the right ideas. Thanks for opening so many doors.

• DuBose Ravenel, M.D., who is living proof that there is such a thing as fate, or synchronicity, or prayers being answered, or whatever you choose to call it. Thanks for getting in touch with me on the very day I needed your letter, and thanks for all your subsequent support and suggestions and your much-needed afterword.

• Judge Graham Mullen, a friend and adviser whose consultation concerning legal issues in the text was invaluable. Thanks for your interest, your time, and your good sense of humor.

• Jeff Koterba, a fine and funny cartoonist as well as a fine and funny fellow. Thanks for adding a much needed "third" dimension to the book.

• Donna Martin, my conscience at Andrews and McMeel, for believing in the book enough to make me write it over again. You're more demanding than my toughest high school English teacher, Donna, and I love you for it.

• Matt Lombardi, my copy editor at Andrews and McMeel, for bringing a cool and exacting eye to the text. You're simply the best practitioner of "The King's English" I've ever had the pleasure of working with, Matt, and I can't thank you enough. (Did I say that right?)

• Willie, my love and my strong light, for supporting me through yet another task that took me away from her. I'm one hell of a lucky guy.

FOREWORD

by Richard Wexler

In 1990, Kmart stores throughout America distributed a special Spider-Man comic book produced by the National Committee to Prevent Child Abuse (NCPCA). The comic, which is still available through NCPCA, stresses that when children are "hit" by their parents they should seek help from another adult, and if the first adult they try won't listen, they should go to another and another until they find one who will. But what does NCPCA mean by "hit"? The comic describes children being beaten up, punched, slapped—and getting a spanking. No distinctions are drawn. In fact, NCPCA opposes "prevention" efforts that distinguish between spanking and physical abuse.

That's because even though at least 88 percent of American children get a spanking now and then, NCPCA and like-minded groups see everything from a spanking to murder as part of a single "continuum" of violence against children. The parent who spanks a child today might well beat him up next week and murder him next year. Never mind that if the continuum theory is true, 88 percent of American children would never reach adulthood.

The comic also tells us that spanking is at the root of all societal violence. Children become classroom bullies, then join street gangs because they were spanked at home when they were small. Never mind that lots of children who don't become antisocial also have been known to receive a spanking now and then.

This Spider-Man comic is but one example of the behavior of the child welfare establishment, people whose nineteenth-century counterparts called themselves "child savers." In 1993, families were victimized by false allegations of child abuse nearly two million times. There are at least a quarter of a million children in foster care who could safely be in their own homes if proper services were provided. But despite already having so much power, the child savers want more. Many of them would like to see spanking outlawed. NCPCA does not officially support such legislation, but it doesn't have to. With efforts like the Spider-Man comic book, NCPCA helps create the climate for such legislation to pass. And such legislation, while not by any means the worst thing that could happen to children, would certainly be more harmful than a swat on the rear end.

The irony of the Great Spanking Debate is that there is a great deal of agreement between John Rosemond and his critics. They agree:
• that children should not be spanked with anything other than an open palm on a clothed bottom;
• that corporal punishment in schools should be banned;
• that spanking should not be used by adults to vent their own frustrations;
• that spanking per se is not an effective means of disciplining children and can, in fact, make their behavior worse.

John Rosemond is bringing sorely needed common sense to this debate. If those who oppose spanking under any and all circumstances could just calm down and read this book, they would learn a great deal about what it takes to raise a happy, secure child. While well-meaning child savers loudly proclaim their "love" for children even as they unintentionally do them harm, the warmth and caring that underlie John Rosemond's approach are apparent on every page. Perhaps that's because John Rosemond is not just an expert—he's also a parent.

The child savers condemn John Rosemond without listening to him. They heap verbal abuse on John for merely assuring parents that one or two swats on the backside can be a good way to stop unacceptable behavior in its tracks and set the stage for the kind of constructive discipline that will help children grow up happy and healthy.

Aha!, the child savers reply. You wouldn't say it was constructive to "hit" an adult under *any* circumstances, now
would you? How is spanking a child any different from as-
saulting a stranger or beating up your spouse?

But the analogy is specious. First, when adults hit each
other, they are attempting to inflict pain. The kind of
spanking John suggests is intended to do nothing of the
sort. Second, children are not adults. That should be obvious enough, but it seems to be lost on many child savers.
We must defend "children's rights," they say. "Children
are not property."

That's true. Children are not property. But they are not
miniature adults, either. Children, especially the very young
children John is talking about, are not capable of reasoning
the way adults can. For toddlers especially, choice can be
an overwhelming burden. To constantly force them to try
to "reason" with adults is an act of mental cruelty, not
kindness.

John Rosemond and I have reached similar conclusions
from very different starting points. As he says in this book,
he is a "social and political conservative." I cast my first
vote for George McGovern and continue to count myself a
liberal. Why then is there so much agreement between
John and myself? I think it's because child saving combines
the very worst elements of liberalism and conservatism: a
faith in unbridled government intervention and a passion
for blaming the victim.

My six-year-old daughter has never been spanked, and I
personally disagree with any spanking that does not follow
the strict, sensible guidelines that John Rosemond advocates in this book. If NCPCA wants to persuade adults to
use other forms of discipline, that's fine. But their Spider-
Man comic isn't aimed at adults. It is addressed to children.
With that publication, NCPCA is going over parents' heads
and interposing themselves and their own child-rearing
biases between parent and child. The comic's underlying
message to children is: Never mind what your parents do

or say, we at NCPCA know what's best for you. If your parents spank you, report them.

Children *should* know that parents don't have a free hand, and that other adults stand ready to help them when they need help. When children are beaten, burned, tortured, or raped by their parents, they need to know that they don't have to put up with it and where to go for protection and help. But to commingle dangers of this sort with spanking is to expose children to serious harm at the hands of their erstwhile saviors.

The Spider-Man comic book, antispanking legislation, and broad, vague laws that confuse poverty with "neglect" all have one thing in common: They devalue family privacy. In this, the Age of Oprah, when all families are presumed "dysfunctional," family privacy is viewed among child savers as virtually synonomous with hiding abuse.

Paul Mones, a lawyer who specializes in defending children who kill their parents, has written that it is wrong for us to "persist in our idealization of the family as an island of peace in a savage, chaotic world." To Mones, family privacy is "the almost pathological desire to maintain parents' control over their children. . . . While we all cherish our right to privacy, we should at the same time realize that our devotion to this cornerstone of democracy is strangling the lives of hundreds of thousands of children and youths every year."

Such rhetoric is all the rage in child-saver circles. It is belied by statistics which show that in any given year, more than 97 percent of American children are *not* abused or neglected. But it also overlooks the fundamental role that family privacy plays in protecting and nurturing children.

In a thousand ways, large and small, parents allow children to grow up healthy and secure by assuring them that the family can and will protect them from outside forces that might hurt them. We parents hardly even stop to think of how often we assure our young children that there is nothing to worry about because Mommy and Daddy are here to protect them. For the overwhelming majority of children, the family is just what the child savers say it is not: "an island of peace in a savage, chaotic world." But almost two million times every year, when they barge in on families where parents have done no wrong, child savers show children that they don't really have this security.

Psychiatrists Anna Freud and Albert Solnit and attorney Joseph Goldstein have written that "the younger the child . . . the stronger is his need to experience his parents as his lawgivers—safe, reliable, all-powerful, and independent." When the child-protective worker comes to the door—often accompanied by police—because someone turned in the parents for spanking and starts interrogating parents and children, that sense of security is immediately undercut. As one parent put it after her child had undergone such an interrogation: "Mother's a fixer in these kids' eyes, [but] Mother couldn't fix it this time. Mother had no power."

And it can be a lot worse. Since child-protective workers have been trained to equate spanking with abuse, the worker may subject the child to a humiliating strip search, looking for bruises. In Illinois, the state's Department of Children and Family Services said in legal papers that even the slightest attempt to regulate strip searches would bring their entire child protective investigative apparatus to a halt—in effect, an admission that strip searching is routine.

Many opponents of spanking also support this kind of unbridled coercive intervention. In contrast, John Rosemond opposes even pulling down a child's pants before a spanking because it is humiliating to the child. One has to wonder: Who's more concerned about protecting children?

Even a strip search may not be the end of it. Protective workers typically come armed with "risk assessment forms" in which points are assigned based on parent behavior and home conditions. Despite the fact that it is perfectly legal to spank a child, on risk assessment forms spanking of any kind is counted as a risk factor. Combine that with a messy home or not enough food in the house or any of the other conditions of poverty that protective workers are trained to confuse with "neglect," and there is an excellent chance that the worker will misuse her "emergency powers" and remove the child from the home on the spot.

A mother whose children were taken for five weeks and then abused in foster care said: "I used to tell the kids, 'You've got nothing to worry about, nobody can ever hurt you, you're safe here with Mom and Dad.' But I can't tell them that anymore."

No, the right to family privacy can't be absolute. But in most cases, trying to preserve such privacy is an act of nurturance by parents, not pathology.

A favorite proverb among child advocates, including some with whom I otherwise agree, is: "It takes a village to raise a child." Vincent Fontana, another leading child saver, quotes with approval an unnamed parish priest who said: "Children do not belong just to their parents; they belong to all of society." Both homilies are wrong. The village can help, but it takes a *parent*—and preferably two—to raise a child. And contrary to Fontana's belief, my daughter does *not* belong to society for one simple reason: Society does not love her. My wife and I do. A psychologist who spoke at a conference I attended a couple of years ago put it this way: "I would not die for my clients," he said. "I would die for my child." And because that is exactly how most parents feel about their children, family privacy is the cornerstone of true child protection.

Richard Wexler is author of Wounded Innocents: The Real Victims of the War Against Child Abuse. *He is Associate Professor of Communications at Penn State University, Beaver Campus, and Vice President of the National Coalition for Child Protection Reform.*

INTRODUCTION

In late November 1993, a Charlotte, N.C., television station carried a feature on spanking during the local segment of the six o'clock news. Although I rarely watch the tube, I happened to be passing through the den when the topic caught my attention. I sat down just in time to hear the newscaster intone—as the message was printed simultaneously across the screen—that when children are spanked: FEAR REPLACES TRUST; PUNISHMENT ESCALATES; VIOLENCE TEACHES VIOLENCE. To underscore these "expert conclusions," a spokesperson from the Chicago-based National Committee for the Prevention of Child Abuse was caught, in soundbite, saying that children who are spanked are likely to "pass it on" by first committing acts of violence on the playground and ultimately within society at large. At the very least, said this ersatz "expert," spanked children grow up burdened with a host of psychological problems, not the least of which is low self-esteem.

At this point, I looked over at my daughter, Amy, whose rear end I had swatted on a handful of occasions during her most petulant middle childhood. I fully expected to see her glaring at me through the remembrance of her victimization; rather, she was rolling her eyes and making lopsidedly lunatic faces to reflect her supposedly distorted psyche. We both giggled.

The problem is, this is far from being funny. Over the last forty years, an antispanking movement has slowly swelled within the so-called "helping" professions. At first, the object was to educate parents to the drawbacks of spanking as well as to more effective means of discipline— laudable goals. This effort has met with limited success, however. Most parents, according to polls, still spank, although generally somewhat less than did *their* parents.

7

There's no indication, furthermore, that professional child-rearing advice has resulted in a better disciplined, and therefore better behaved, generation of children. In fact, there are definite signs that American parents are becoming increasingly disenchanted with professional child-rearing advice in general and are once again embracing—as yours truly has been encouraging for years—good old-fashioned common sense and intuition.

That growing numbers of parents are refusing to heed professional advice concerning the dos and don'ts of discipline—and spanking in particular—is a source of increasing frustration to social activists within the helping professions. Their frustration and zealotry are now driving a movement to make spankings illegal, as is already the case in Sweden. These professionals (along with influential converts within the lay community) reason that if parents will not voluntarily stop doing something that is—in their parochial view—damaging to children, then it is necessary that they be *made*—as in legally enjoined—to stop.

In recent years, the major media have gravitated to the political correctness of the antispanking movement, advancing its platform and lending significantly to the public perception that its claims are indeed credible, nay, irrefutable. The problem is, they are not credible. They are bankrupt. There is absolutely no worthwhile evidence to support the notion that children who are occasionally (the operative word) spanked stop trusting their parents and begin fearing them instead; no reason to believe that parents who spank are certain to do so more often and more severely over time; nothing but thin air supporting the claim that spankings induct children into a "culture of violence"; nothing but rhetoric behind the notion that spankings per se engender psychological problems. These claims are inventions, myths; but they are far from harmless.

A Brief History

In the 1960s, helping professionals began actively promoting a child-rearing philosophy which holds that parent and child are equals—not in theory, mind you, but in *fact*. According to psychologist Thomas Gordon, one of the chief architects of the democratic family movement and author of *Parent Effectiveness Training* (1970), or *P.E.T.*, one of the all-time best-sellers in the parenting field, parents should treat children as they would treat adult friends. (*P.E.T.*, page 213: "[Gordon's method of conflict resolution] is treating kids much as we treat friends or a spouse. The method feels so good to children because they like so much to feel trusted and to be treated as an equal.") Parental authority, according to Gordon, his followers and heirs, is arbitrary and repressive, if not downright abusive. Its very exercise (which includes telling children, in no uncertain terms, what they can do, cannot do, and must do, and punishing them when they disobey) is an insidious form of psychological violence against the child. More specifically, the traditional exercise of parental authority damages a child's *self-esteem*—a nebulous ether which accumulates in a child's psyche as adults strive to "make the child feel good about himself."

By the mid-1970s, these *nouveau* ideas concerning the politics of the parent-child relationship had become the "party line" within psychology and related professions. "Low self-esteem" became the standard explanation for nearly all problems of childhood. The implication behind this pseudo-diagnosis was that a problem child's parents were unenlightened throwbacks, needing parent "education." As this mythology became ever more widely accepted by lay and professional alike, so did the notion that traditional—call them old-fashioned—forms of discipline, even if they did not result in bruises, were harmful and therefore de facto forms of abuse. With the help of the media, the professional community succeeded in convincing significant numbers of Americans that whole previous generations of parents had controlled their children by means of psychologically destructive disciplinary techniques. At a wholesale level, parents of previous generations were made out to be villains who created "dysfunctional families" and rained abuse upon their children. If this abuse was not intrusive, as in its sexual and physical forms, then it was certainly psychological. In any case, for society to advance to its "next stage of evolution," traditional child-rearing methods had to go. It was from this stage that antispankers began advancing their platform.

(The propaganda effort to demonize parents of previous generations is very much alive and well today. In an article which appeared in the January 1993 issue of *Lears* magazine, family counselor and best-selling author John Bradshaw wrote: "My thesis is that any of us who were raised in the traditional patriarchal system have trouble relating because we've been 'mystified' to some degree by an upbringing that compels obedience and rules by fear, a raising that can be survived only by denial of the authentic self.")

Word Games

The very language of the antispanking movement is disingenuous. It's spokepersons rarely use the word *spanking*. Instead, they talk in terms of "hitting" or "striking" or "beating." Parents who spank, they say, are "physically attacking" their children. Swatting a child's rear is referred to as an "act of violence" which supposedly teaches children that hitting is a justifiable response to someone who makes you upset. Spankings also *confuse* children, they claim. How, they ask, can children possibly be expected to understand that although their parents can hit them, they cannot turn around and hit their parents? With rhetoric of this sort, antispankers seek to create the impression that a beating and a spanking are one and the same; that swatting (a term they do not use, either) a child's rear end is no different, in the final analysis, from slapping a child in the face. They are both acts of child abuse—equally violent, equally damaging to the child and society. One's just more likely to leave a visible mark, that's all.

This amounts to nothing more than misleading propaganda. The purpose is to create a climate of acceptance for the passage of legislation which will turn the majority of parents into criminals of the most heinous kind—those whose victims are defenseless children. The resulting body of law will play directly into the hands of ultraliberal social engineers as well as social activists within the professional community. The outward motive—the protection of children—conceals several more insidious ones:

• The desire to expand and consolidate the power of the helping professions. At the present time, there is no law that says an individual *must,* under certain circumstances, submit to psychological evaluation and counseling. If they are written as is being suggested, however, antispanking laws will require exactly that. They will give helping professionals the power to define when the law has been broken, who is in need of "help" and how much, and when a certain parent's "rehabilitation" is complete. It is significant to note that in all of history the only other state to confer this much power on psychologists and their ilk was the former Soviet Union.

• The desire to manipulate the inner workings of the American family; specifically, the desire to exercise significant control over the child-rearing process. Take it from someone who was, at one time, similarly guilty, a significant number of helping professionals possess a "save the world" mentality. They believe they know what's best for individuals, families, and children. The only problem, as they see it, is that most people are "in denial"—unwilling to recognize their need for help. This self-righteousness fuels a zealous, missionary attitude. And like the first missionaries to the New World, many helping professionals seem

to believe that their vision of a perfect world justifies whatever means they deem necessary, including licensing parents, taking children away from parents they define as unfit, and the like. (For a close look at the social engineering being proposed by some professionals, see *Debating Children's Lives,* Mason and Gambrill, eds., Sage Publications, 1994).

• Antispanking laws would solve a nagging problem for Child Protective Service agencies nationwide: to wit, the criticism that current child abuse and neglect laws discriminate against the poor—that, in fact, definitions of neglect and abuse are often synonomous with definitions of poverty. A prohibition on spanking would be nondiscriminatory; it would "tie the hands," so to speak, of haves and have-nots alike. After all, the typical *Fortune* 500 CEO has probably never beaten his children in ways that produced bruises on their bodies; nevertheless, he has probably spanked them. Antispanking laws would mean that he would be no less vulnerable to the forced "interventions" of Child Protective Services workers than an unemployed single mother of three living hand-to-mouth in a slum tenement.

I have written this book in order to awaken as many as possible to the threat antispanking legislation poses to the integrity and autonomy of the American family and, as such, the very survival of individual freedom. If that sounds overblown, you need only understand that the successful passage of a law against spanking will open a set of legislative floodgates. If parents can be prohibited from spanking, what's next? The same justifications being used to advance antispanking laws—that spanking does psychological harm to children—can also be used to justify prohibiting other forms of punishment, including strong verbal reprimands, banishing children to their rooms, grounding teens for extended periods of time, and so on. If you think that a law against verbally reprimanding a child is beyond the pale of possibility, consider that just a generation ago, parents would have said that a law prohibiting a parent from swatting a child's rear end was not possible in America; that after all, *this* was a free country. Antispanking laws will be a foot in the door to grander schemes, believe me.

But Not If I Can Help It

There is absolutely no doubt about it, we need laws which, as much as possible, protect children from actual, quantifiable abuse and provide for the punishment of their tormentors. But beating and spanking are apples and oranges. One of my purposes in this book is to draw a clear distinction between the one and the other. In the view of those who would have spankings outlawed, however, I am, by attempting to make such a distinction, "giving permission to parents who abuse their children"—an accusation that's been leveled at me on numerous occasions. This sort of rhetoric is revealing of zealotry, an inability to think clearly when it comes to this issue.

Do I believe parents *should* spank their children? No, I do not. I believe that parents should discipline themselves and their children such that children are instilled with functional moral values and an abiding sense of responsibility concerning their own behavior. As the reader who ventures further will discover, I do *not* believe that in and of themselves spankings *correct* misbehavior. In this sense, a spanking is an extremely ineffective consequence. Parents who mistakenly believe otherwise cannot understand why, no matter how often or hard they spank, the misdeeds in question keep occurring. Are spankings good for anything? Yes, they certainly are. What, pray tell? Read on.

Despite what proponents of antispanking laws would have you believe, the evidence is *not* on their side. Properly administered (the operative condition!), spankings do not, as the media cooperatively announce, cause children to lose trust in and become fearful of their parents. I hope to convince you, beyond a shadow of doubt, of that. I also intend to convince you that properly administered spankings do not, as a matter of course, escalate in severity or cause children to become violent, either on the playground or in later life. Last, but by no means least, I'll give suggestions on ways of following up on spankings so as to insure their effectiveness. In spanking as in a golf swing, the follow-through is all-important.

To begin with, here are some facts (a confession, if you will): My wife and I spanked both of our children. Not often, but when we did, it was memorable. At this writing, Eric is twenty-five, married to the daughter-in-law of our dreams, and employed as a corporate pilot. Amy is twenty-two, finishing college, and looking forward to a career in marketing and public relations. Neither child exhibits any antisocial tendencies. Beyond typically youthful anxieties concerning the future (and with consideration of the fact that the condition of being human *is* a psycho-spiritual problem), neither child exhibits emotional problems. Notwithstanding a relatively brief period of time to the contrary during early adolescence (when neither of them would so much as acknowledge our existence), both children have always trusted us, communicated well with us, and been very affectionate toward us. And the same things can be said for the overwhelming majority of spanked children—past, present, and future.

In short, the claims of the antispanking movement are absurdly simplistic. It takes more than spankings to make a bully, much less a criminal. It takes a lot more than an occasional swat or two on the butt to warp a child's mind. The bond of trust between parent and child will endure emotional upheavals far greater than spankings can produce. Unfortunately, simplistic arguments are often extremely seductive.

To agree with the antispanking position carries no risk—professional or otherwise—whereas disagreement does. In the minds of many antispankers, to disagree with them makes one an enemy of children, a de facto child abuser. To illustrate, shortly after I wrote a newspaper column in which I said that a properly administered spanking is no big deal, a family therapist wrote me a letter saying that, in her estimation, I was in "obvious need of help." In other words: we disagree; therefore, I must have "issues" that I need to "resolve."

Also complicating any discussion of this issue is the belief—usually associated with Christian fundamentalism—that spankings with "rods" of one sort or another are necessary to successful discipline. I happen to be a social and political conservative and I am also a Christian, but I must admit to having great difficulty with the notion that belts, switches, and paddles, laid on with gusto, are needed to propel the oft-recalcitrant child down the road to righteousness. In the chapters that follow, I will examine the biblical side of the spanking issue as well. I hope the "solution" I propose will be ecumenically acceptable.

Regardless, I'm confident that conservatively minded fellow Christians will not be up in arms over what I have to say in the following pages. But the movers and shakers in the antispanking movement will be. Being zealots, they will be thrown into a nuclear tizzy by my critique of their misguided, ill-intentioned goal. They will see this book as a declaration of war, which in a sense it is. Actually, the war is already being fought, on many fronts, by many good people. I'm referring to the culture war in which America is currently embroiled—in which the clash you hear is that between the rhetoric of avant-garde philosophies and the voice of reason. This book is about one of the battles in that war.

So, it's off to war I go. Will you join me?

Chapter One

To
Spare
or Not to
Spare

PART ONE:
SPARING THE ROD

In the spring of 1993, in a hotel room somewhere in America and desperate for the sound of a human voice, I turned on the television. Up popped Oprah, who was orchestrating a politically correct hoot 'n' holler over spanking. I know how these things work because I've been on several such free-for-alls (never again, I assure you). The producer, acting on behalf of the host, assembles a panel of people who are expected, perhaps even coached, to express a certain opinion. The illusion of "balance" is quickly dispelled as one realizes the host has an agenda. In this case, Ms. Winfrey's clearly was to promote to public acceptance the idea that the act of spanking is, without exception, child abuse and should be made illegal. That's right, as in *against the law*!

At one point in this ersatz discussion, Oprah approached a man in the audience whom I immediately pegged as a "plant." This very professional-looking gentleman, in re-

sponse to a rogue's gallery of parents who had all con-
fessed to spanking their children (and their intention to
continue doing so), reeled off something to the effect that
spankings instill a violent bent into the psyches of children
and, furthermore, amount to a mixed message. The fact
that parents can hit a child, yet the child cannot hit them
back, he said, is horribly confusing and destructive to self-
esteem. The audience roared on cue, Oprah smiled know-
ingly, and all was well in Talk Show Land.

With this scene fresh in mind, I subsequently asked the
250 members of an audience in Pueblo, Colorado, "Please
raise a hand if you were spanked as a child." Close to 250
hands went up. "Now," I continued, "keep your hand up if
you remember that as a child you were confused over or
resented the fact that although your parents felt free to
spank you, you were not allowed to hit them." Immediately,
all hands went down.

I replicated this demonstration with several other audi-
ences that same spring. The results were always the same.
I occasionally tacked on the request that those who were
spanked as kids raise their hands again if they ever recall
feeling that the fact their parents spanked them meant that
hitting someone in anything other than self-defense was
okay. Never once did anyone raise a hand. Either the people who attend my presentations are atypical, or the politically correct rhetoric concerning the effects of spanking
on children is dead wrong.

I've seen the research on spanking. In fact, this being
a relatively fascinating topic, I dare say I've kept closely
abreast of the research. Some of it paints an ominous pic-
ture: A person who was spanked as a child is more likely to
commit violent crimes as an adult, be physically abusive toward his or her spouse and children, suffer from low self-
esteem . . . in short, become a misfit in every possible sense.

One of the most outspoken, oft-quoted critics of spanking is sociologist Murray Straus of the University of New
Hampshire Family Research Laboratory. Straus's opinions

Behind the scenes at a politically correct TV talk show...

have significantly informed and shaped the rhetoric of the antispanking movement. In fact, it can legitimately be said that he is its "guru."

In a 1994 article (which appears in *Debating Children's Lives*, Mason and Gambrill, eds., Sage Publications), Dr. Straus asserts that "research showing the harmful effects of spanking is one of the best-kept secrets of American child psychology" because it implies that "almost all American parents are guilty of child abuse, *including those who write books of advice for parents* [emphasis mine, and yes, I stand accused]."

Citing a study which found that nearly all parents of toddlers spank, more than half of parents of teens spank, and 41 percent of parents feel a spanking is appropriate in the case of a child hitting another child, Straus says these parents send their children a double message: Hitting another person is bad, but it is not bad to hit someone who's done something bad. His conclusion: "Corporal punishment therefore teaches the morality of hitting."

Another aspect of spanking's "hidden curriculum," as Straus calls the supposedly irrevocable lessons he sees embedded in the act of swatting a child's rear end, is the message "those who love you, hit you." Spankings also teach, says Straus, that it is "morally acceptable to hit those you love when they 'do wrong.'" This aspect of the "hidden curriculum" is "almost a recipe for violence between spouses later in life."

After citing the results of surveys which supposedly demonstrate that spankings place children at greater risk for eventual criminal behavior, alcoholism, suicide, drug use, and lower occupational achievement, Straus comes to his point, which is a call for laws prohibiting the spanking of children *under any circumstances*. Straus firmly believes that antispanking laws will result in a "healthier, less violent, wealthier" society. He points to the fact that spanking has been against the law in Sweden since 1979. (For quite some time, Sweden has been plagued with alarmingly high rates of alcoholism, divorce, and illegitimacy. These long-standing crises, which are a direct result of Sweden's socialist politics, have contributed greatly to unusually high levels of stress in Swedish families—many of which are single-parent. As a result, Sweden's child abuse rate was—and continues to be—relatively high, prompting passage of an antispanking law which has not been shown to have reduced child abuse one iota.)

Straus proposes, however, that parents who violate these proposed laws should *not* be punished. Rather, as is the case in Sweden, the fact that they spank their children should be taken as a sign they need help, and the help should be provided. In fact, the "help" Straus refers to amounts to forced intervention into the family on the part of the state. In the case of parents who refuse this "help," the state will then be free to take clearly punitive measures, all under the guise of protecting the children, including removing them from the home, possibly permanently.

Straus's research and conclusions are full of gaping holes:
• First, his studies fail to demonstrate that spankings per se cause any problems—psychological, behavioral, or otherwise. His conclusions are based in large part on data collected from adults who report having been spanked *as teenagers*. Straus claims to have discovered that the more frequently a person was spanked as a teen, the more likely it is that as an adult that person will assault his wife, abuse his or her children, use alcohol to problematic excess, and think about committing suicide. But the mere fact that parents are spanking a teenager, and frequently at that, suggests that the teen's behavior may already be antisocial. At the very least, it speaks of serious family problems. In other words, rather than proving a link between spanking and later antisocial behavior, Straus simply demonstrates what common sense will tell us: that spankings at this age are a red flag indicating that serious problems already exist in the teen's life—in other words, that he or she

is "at risk." To extend this line of thinking: We might also discover that in addition to being frequently spanked as teens, lots of criminals, wife beaters, etc., cannot remember ever being hugged or kissed or told they were loved by their parents. In that case, what "caused" their later anti-social behavior? Being spanked as children? Being starved of affection? We'll never know. All we know is that these individuals didn't have happy childhoods and that an unhappy childhood is predictive of later problems. Common sense.

• A second major problem with Straus's conclusions is that he fails—as is the case with all of the research I've ever seen that reaches blanket antispanking conclusions—to distinguish between a *beating* and a *spanking*. In effect, Straus and other antispankers feel that such a distinction does not exist. In their view, the moment a parent strikes a child—regardless of where on the child's body the strike lands, regardless of the force behind the strike, regardless of whether the parent uses a hand or some other implement, such as a belt—the parent has committed child abuse. Period. As a result of Straus's unwillingness to distinguish between a beating and a spanking (a difference which will be clearly spelled out in the next chapter), his results are skewed to the negative by the life histories of people who, as children, suffered unspeakable abuse. No doubt about it, if you're beaten on as a child, you're more likely, as an adult, to pass it on. This, too, is common sense.

• Straus's spanking-leads-to-wife-beating hypothesis is contradicted by the fact that whereas the overwhelming majority of males in my generation were spanked as children, the number who beat their wives is extremely small, albeit problematic. This is yet another example of Straus's overall tendency to oversimplify extremely complex social situations, a trait that is hardly conducive to conducting worthwhile sociological study.

• Straus cannot even come close to proving his claim that spanking's "hidden curriculum" teaches children that "those who love you, hit you" and that violence is a just response to a maddening social situation. This is rhetoric, pure and simple. It is, however, emotionally seductive (which is, after all, the point of rhetoric), but in the final analysis it is nothing more than undiluted psychobabble—a construction of language, not of fact.

• Straus and other antispankers frequently argue that parents always have options other than to spank. That goes without saying, but again, the existence of other options doesn't prove that spanking is abusive or even ineffective. The question is whether any of the options, in any given situation, would be as effective as a spanking or in combination *with* a spanking. Psychologist Robert Larzelere, director of research at a residential treatment facility for children and youth and an adjunct faculty member of the University of Iowa, has found that the effectiveness of two frequently mentioned disciplinary options—verbal reprimand and time-out—actually *improves* in combination with a mild spanking, expecially with children between the ages of two and six. This suggests, says Larzelere, that parents who enhance their discipline with occasional *mild* spankings during their children's earlier years may have better-behaved teens. That is certainly consistent with my own observations.

• Straus also makes the mistake of taking spanking out of context of a parent's total disciplinary style. A very well-known study which sought to determine the outcomes of various parenting styles found that children of *authoritative* parents—characterized by firm control and high nurturance—were more socially responsible and exercised greater individual initiative than children of either permissive (low control, high nurturance) or authoritarian (excessive control, low nurturance) parents. *Authoritative* parents, furthermore, were generally willing to occasionally spank. The conclusion reached was that spanking per se was not harmful, but rather that the *total pattern* of parental behavior was of utmost importance in determining the effectiveness of any disciplinary method, including spanking.

Having been trained in the scientific method, Straus is well aware that his research proves nothing. The fact that he pretends it does reveals the lack of objectivity he brings to this issue. In further fact, it suggests that Straus (and this is a problem common to antispanking "research") isn't doing research at all. He's attempting to promote a point of view. In effect, Straus is cloaking a propaganda effort in the trappings of "science."

In an interview with the *Philadelphia Inquirer* (November 1993), Straus identifies several "myths" concerning spanking, including: *I was spanked and I'm okay.* After pointing out that a *small* percentage of spanked children experience harmful effects, he asks, "Why chance it?" Again, Straus is wrong. It is *not* a myth that the overwhelming majority of people who were spanked as kids are okay as adults. In fact, he disproves his own contention by admitting that the number who do not turn out okay is small. (Keep in mind that Straus does not distinguish between a beating and a spanking. Therefore, it's probably correct to assume that the small percentage of children he refers to as being harmed come primarily from the ranks of those who were beaten.) To cite my personal example, I was spanked as a kid. I'm comfortable with myself, enjoy positive relations with my wife, children, and friends, and am satisfyingly productive. (Straus might say, however, that the fact I spanked my children proves I'm not okay at all.) In fact, I was often spanked with a belt. So was my wife. We're both okay. We spanked both of our children (albeit never with anything other than our hands), and the evidence is overwhelmingly in favor of concluding that both of our kids, as young adults, are very okay. The same can be said for the vast majority of people who were spanked as children. Straus asks, "Why chance it?" I ask, if the risk is—by his own admission—small, and the connection between being spanked and developing later problems is tenuous, and we already have laws concerning the blatant abuse of children, why do we need a law against spanking? Straus's argument here is akin to proposing that since a small number of people die during heart transplants, heart transplants should be made illegal.

Most people would, no doubt, agree that certain instances of parents striking children are, indeed, abusive. Likewise, verbal reprimands can be abusive. According to the "logic" of the antispanking argument, in the interest of not "chancing it," we should ban the use of all "negative language" when addressing children. Or, since confining a child to his room may put the child at greater risk for claustrophobia, parents should be prohibited, by law, from exercising this "more risky" form of discipline. To some degree—at least at present—these scenarios are nothing more than absurd parodies of the antispanking mentality. I for one, however, am becoming increasingly convinced that we're talking about people who, if given an inch in the social policy realm, will want a mile. These are, I fear, social engineers of the worst kind, itching to impose their influence upon the American family.

According to Straus and his cohorts in the antispanking movement, slapping a child's rear end is abuse. Only the enlightened few see through the wall of denial American parents—with the assistance of many child-rearing authorities—have erected to shield themselves from this national disgrace. Since the rest of us are unwilling to admit the error of our ways (or our advice!), the only option is to pass laws which will turn the average parent into a criminal. Not to worry, however, because offending parents won't be punished. They will be given "help." And who, pray tell, will provide this help? Why "helping professionals," of course. I think it's safe to assume that these individuals, despite their altruistic mission, will expect to be compensated for their services.

The possibility of such legislation raises a host of very conceivable possibilities, none of which is consistent with democratic principles or the privacy and stability of families. I can envision, for example, "family living education" classes in schools which would have the intended effect of encouraging children to report instances of having been "mis-parented," including having been spanked. At present, there is hardly an elementary school counselor in America who has not had a child complain that a mild spanking from his or her parents was, in the child's immature mind, abusive. Imagine the number of children who will line up outside the offices of school counselors around the country if the day comes that even a mild a spanking is, by legal definition, abuse.

Along these lines, the National Committee to Prevent Child Abuse recently published (with funds from Kmart Corporation) a Spider-Man comic book in which Spider-Man helps a father see that one reason his son is getting into fights at school is because the boy is receiving spankings at home. On page 5, Spider-Man tells the youngster that any time he is "hit" he should tell a grown-up, and keep on telling grown-ups until he finds someone who will listen and do something about it. On page 6, a spanking from a parent is equated with hitting.

In a letter to me, Richard Wexler, author of *Wounded Innocents* (Prometheus Books, 1990), had this to say about Spider-Man's message:

> Now imagine this scenario: A child gets a spanking and, following Spider-Man's advice, tells his teacher he's been "hit" by his parent. The teacher is required to report any suspicion of "child abuse." She makes such a report and a caseworker is sent to the home to investigate. . . . At a minimum, the child is in for a traumatic interrogation and, quite possibly, a strip-search as the worker looks for bruises. At worst, the worker will remove the child [from the home] on the spot.

By the time the book you hold in your hands is published, NCPCA's Spider-Man comic will have been distributed to thousands of children in public schools across America and discussed in many a classroom.

Amazingly enough, NCPCA denies that one of the intents of the comic is to equate spanking with abuse. During an April 1994 phone conversation and in a subsequent letter, Ann Cohn Donnelly, NCPCA's executive director, assured me they have no official position favoring anti-spanking legislation and do not feel that spankings per se are abusive. When I pointed out that their Spider-Man comic not only equates being spanked by parents with being "hit" by peers or teachers and suggests that children who are spanked should report their parents to authorities, Donnelly replied that "some people might interpret it that way" but denied that the comic was meant to imply that any and all spankings administered by parents are inappropriate. Donnelly was being evasive. The comic's introduction, written by her and addressed to children, reads:

> The stories you are about to read are about hitting and why we believe that people are not for hitting— and children are people, too. The stories are about children who are being hit by adults they know or by other children. They tell you what to do if someone is hitting you. Perhaps you or someone you know has been the object of someone else's violence. . . .

Nowhere does the comic differentiate between being slapped in the face by, say, a teacher and being spanked on the buttocks by a parent. Quite the contrary, they are both examples of "hitting." In either case, says NCPCA, the child in question should tell adults until one listens. Regardless of Donnelly's disclaimer, the message to children reading the comic is clear: If your parents spank you, you should report them to other adult authority figures.

According to Richard Wexler, NCPCA has consistently refused to distinguish between physical abuse and corporal punishment and has gone on record as opposing any effort to do so. According to NCPCA, any statement that

might be construed as condoning spanking "doesn't belong in a child abuse prevention presentation."

In 1990, NCPCA published a brochure entitled "How to Teach Your Children Discipline." It states that spanking is not a useful approach to discipline because it "is used to directly control children's behavior," teaches children "to solve problems by hitting others," and teaches children "to be afraid of the adult in charge." The brochure also implies that spankings are violent acts of "lashing out" by parents who are out of control.

Strictly speaking, Ann Cohn Donnelly is correct. NCPCA has never *explicitly* stated that spankings and child abuse are one and the same, but it is equally true that they have never taken any pains to distinguish between spankings and behaviors which are clearly abusive, such as slapping, punching, kicking, etc. Furthermore, as Richard Wexler points out, they refuse to do so, citing as rationale the sort of "data" generated by Murray Straus and like-minded ideologues. NCPCA's position statement on physical punishment, adopted May 1989, reads:

> Although physical punishment of children is prevalent in the United States, numerous studies have demonstrated that hitting, spanking, slapping, and other forms of physical punishment are harmful methods of changing children's behavior. . . .

Ignoring for the moment the fact that this statement is not true, the tone and content of NCPCA's propaganda clearly leads to the conclusion that spanking a child on the buttocks is in the final analysis no different from slapping the child in the face.

Donnelly also told me that she didn't think antispanking legislation would ever fly in the United States because it would be regarded as too intrusive. That's true, but again, she's being disingenuous. At the present time, NCPCA knows that it would be political suicide for any legislator, state or national, to sponsor a law *specifically prohibiting parental spanking.* The prohibition, should it ever come, will more likely be the result of a judicial ruling rather than a legislative act. A group calling itself The National Task Force for Children's Constitutional Rights (NTFCCR), whose advisory board consists of a number of prominent individuals from the fields of law, psychology, medicine, and family social work, believes that the best way to protect children from mistreatment within their own families is through an amendment to the Constitution of the United States. The proposed wording of this amendment would open a judicial Pandora's box that could well lead to antispanking rulings in the courts:

> Section 1
> All citizens of the United States who are fifteen years of age or younger shall enjoy the right to live in a home that is safe and healthy . . . and the right to the care of a loving family or a substitute thereof. . . .

One of NTFCCR's cofounders, Connecticut Superior Court Judge Charles D. Gill, gives approximately fifty speeches a year in which he issues the clarion call for a children's rights movement to be modeled on the women's movement. In a 1991 article for the *Ohio Northern University Law Review,* Gill equates a Children's Rights Amendment with the Equal Rights Amendment. Conceding that ERA was defeated, he notes that "nearly half of our states have enacted an Equal Rights Amendment" and "nearly all state legislatures have passed legislation that alters the status of women."

In other words, Gill is saying that while a Children's Rights Amendment to the Constitution might not fly at present, it might be possible to galvanize enough public support behind such a concept to implement its equivalent on a state-by-state basis. If such legislation is eventually enacted, it would only be a matter of time before an attorney acting on behalf of a child would file a suit asserting that a parent who spanks is failing to provide a "safe, healthy, and loving" environment, thus violating the child's protected rights. If a judge concurred, a de facto law prohibiting parental spanking would be on the books.

Support for a Children's Rights Amendment is growing. In 1991, the National Committee for the Rights of the Child (NCRC) was formed in Washington, D.C. According to Judge Gill, dozens of national groups, representing millions of Americans, met to initiate "The Next Great Movement in America."

The United Nations is even in on the act. In 1989, the UN Convention on the Rights of the Child was unanimously adopted. Article 19 of its charter states: "Parties shall take all appropriate legislative, administrative, social and educational measures to protect the child from all forms of physical or mental violence, injury or abuse . . . while in the care of parents, legal guardians or any other person who has the care of the child." While this does not specifically define spanking as "physical violence," the intent of the framers is to include parental spanking in that rather broad category. (Radda Barnen—Sweden's Save the Children—was intimately involved in drafting and implementing the Swedish law banning parental spanking as well as in drafting the wording of Article 19 of the UN Convention on the Rights of the Child.) The convention went into force as international law on September 2, 1990, when it was ratified by the twentieth nation. Close to one hundred nations have now ratified, thus affirming that they are legally bound by its standards. One notable holdout: the United States of America.

But an international organization calling itself End Physical Punishment of Children (EPOCH) is working diligently to enlighten American diplomats and lawmakers as to the rights of children. EPOCH's worldwide aim is that of "ending all physical punishment of children by education and legal reform." In their literature, they state that "hitting children is a violation of their fundamental rights as people and a constant confirmation of their low status," and they make it perfectly clear that spanking is hitting. As of 1992, EPOCH was able to boast that largely as a result of their efforts, physical punishment of children by parents had been legally proscribed in Sweden, Finland, Denmark, Norway, and Austria. In addition, similar bills are up for consideration in Germany, the United Kingdom, Canada, and Bolivia.

Completing the circle, the cofounder of the American chapter of EPOCH, Adrienne Hauser, is on National Staff at the National Committee to Prevent Child Abuse. (During the writing of this book, I left several messages asking Ms. Hauser to call me, but she never responded.) So although NCPCA may publicly disavow support for antispanking legislation, strong connections exist between themselves and organizations like EPOCH, the National Committee for the Rights of Children, and the National Task Force for Children's Constitutional Rights, which are working toward that end.

As reflected in much of NCPCA's literature, the distinct possibility exists that antispanking legal rulings would be just one stage in the ever-broadening legal definition of child abuse. Once spankings are defined as abusive, it's quite conceivable that raising one's voice to a child (yelling) would be next on the list of parenting behaviors to be deemed abusive (in a letter which appeared in "Dear Abby" in April of 1994, Joy Byers, an NCPCA spokesperson, writes: "Never raise your voice, or your hand, in anger.") followed by banishing a child to his or her room. (If you think the latter prospect is absurd, think again. A considerable number of helping professionals are presently of the opinion that restricting a child to his room causes the development of "negative feelings" concerning what should be a "positive environment," thus increasing the risk of onset of separation anxieties, phobias, sleep disturbances, and the like, not to mention lowered self-esteem.)

Where does this end? The answer: It doesn't, for it is the inherent nature of institutional bureaucracies not only to perpetuate themselves but to expand their influence—their "mandate"—within society. As child abuse laws are liberalized, it is inevitable that the numbers of children removed from their homes and placed in the care of the state would increase, as would the number of terminations of parental rights. As one concerned reader of my syndicated newspaper column recently wrote: "I am genuinely frightened concerning the attempts of well-intentioned social engineers to effect the 'redistribution' of children to 'better' parents. The ultimate outcome is the destruction of the family as we know it." Paranoia? Keep in mind that just forty years ago, the average citizen would have regarded someone who warned of the coming of antispanking laws as nothing less than hysterical, in both senses of the term.

Murray Straus says that, under his proposed legislation, parents who spanked would not be punished, only helped. That's if, and only if, they admitted they needed help. What if, as a matter of principle, a parent refused to make such a confession? At present, if a parent clearly abuses a child and refuses to admit that his or her actions toward the child are wrong, the child is almost always immediately removed from the home until the parent's discipline has undergone successful rehabilitation. The very real possibility that this policy would be extended to parents who administer mild spankings yet refuse to confess the error of their ways is downright scary.

Straus tells us that antispanking laws will transform us into a "healthier, less violent, and wealthier society." This grand vision serves to distract from the more insidious aspects of such laws, including that for many otherwise law-abiding American parents, receiving professional "help" would no longer be a matter of choice. In short, the specter raised is one of a totalitarian family policy, one that puts the autonomy of the American family at tremendous risk.

There is evidence, furthermore, that an antispanking

law might be profoundly counterproductive. It is significant to note that the outlawing of spanking in Sweden may
have actually *increased* the incidence of child abuse. One
study—done a year after Sweden enacted antispanking
laws—found that the Swedish rate of beating a child or
threatening to use or using a weapon of some sort against a
child was *two to four times that of the rate in the United States.*
This is especially telling of the ultimate effect of antispanking laws, since Sweden is by other measures a far less
violent society than the United States. Their murder rate,
for example, is less than half that of our own. To explain
this paradox, psychologist Larzelere posits that occasional
mild spankings may serve as a safety valve of sorts, preventing escalations of misbehavior and parental frustration of the sort that lead to physical explosions. He further
suggests—and I second his emotion—that providing parents who intend to spank with guidelines for spanking appropriately and effectively may do more to reduce child
abuse than laws which prohibit spanking altogether.

When all is said and done, this argument isn't about
spanking; it's about people, zealous professionals, politics,
and political correctness. It's about people who feel morally superior and therefore justified in their desire to impose their ideology on everyone, by hook or crook. The
more frustrated they become, the more outrageous and
dangerous they become. That's the problem with moral
superiority in any form. Frustrated, it inclines toward
totalitarianism.

The problem with spanking is not spanking per se.
Again, it's people—people who use corporal punishment
inappropriately. It's a people problem that will *not* be
solved through legislation. It will, in all likelihood, never
be completely solved, only mitigated. It can be mitigated
through education. So let's begin the education, keeping
in mind that the best, most effective educators, the ones
that cause people to truly want to listen, inquire, and learn,
don't promote extremist points of view.

PART TWO:
SPOILING THE CHILD

Also relevant to a thorough discussion of spanking is the view often espoused by those who believe that every word of Scripture should be taken literally—a view that has become associated with the phrase "spare the rod, spoil the child." (It often surprises people to learn that "spare the rod, spoil the child" is not to be found anywhere in the Bible. In fact, it is a rather licentious paraphrase of Proverbs 13:24 by seventeenth-century English poet Samuel Butler. In all likelihood, Butler was referring to the "canings" which were then common in English boarding schools.)

This "use the rod" position draws primarily from two relatively isolated biblical passages: Proverbs 13:24 ("He who spares his rod, hates his son, / But he who loves him disciplines him diligently") and Proverbs 23:13 ("Do not hold back discipline from the child, / Although you beat him with the rod, he will not die"). The belief is that these passages are explicitly instructive; that a child's original, "sinful" nature cannot be overcome gently, but only by forceful spankings with "rods" of one sort or another, including belts, switches, and paddles.

To begin with, the idea that there is no room for interpretation when seeking to understand God's word is a minority view in Judeo-Christian circles and contradicted by the fact that most of Jesus' teachings were in parable, replete with metaphor—the language of the spiritual subconscious. In effect, Jesus often spoke obliquely, and those who misunderstood him—including the Pharisees—were those very people who tended to take everything He said literally. The word of God comes "alive" when we accept the challenge to search out its many, many levels of meaning.

As metaphor, the biblical "rod" can justly be interpreted as a symbol of parental authority, just as in ancient days the scepter was the symbol of a ruler's authority and the staff the symbol of a priest's. The rod is also a traditional and ancient measure of length, and as such means that parents should define clear limits for their children. Being a strong, straight stick, the rod is also a metaphor for firmness and consistency in discipline. The same term is also used elsewhere in the Bible in an obviously figurative sense (e.g., Psalm 2:9: "Thou shalt break them with a rod of iron; / Thou shalt shatter them like earthenware").

As regards Proverbs 23:13, one might ask, What kind of "rod" can a child be beaten with and yet stand absolutely no chance of dying? After all, if an adult slave might possibly die from having been beaten with a rod (e.g., Exodus 21:20: "And if a man strikes his male or female slave with a rod and he dies at his hand, he shall be punished"), then why not a small child, pray tell? One way, perhaps the only way, of reconciling this apparent contradiction is to assume that the rod of Proverbs is not a stick at all, but rather a metaphor, representing steadfast discipline in many forms.

Even if scriptural references to the rod are taken literally, there is hardly justification for taking them out of context. Whereas one of the four Hebrew words for *rod* can, indeed, mean a large, threatening implement (e.g., Exodus 21:20), the word used in Proverbs is also used in Isaiah 28:27 to suggest a relatively flimsy instrument used to thresh caraway *so as not to damage it*. In this regard, it is interesting to note that threshing is the process of separating the useful part of the grain from its chaff. Applied to child rearing, this yields the metaphor of discipline as the prolonged process of separating useful behaviors from those which are of no use. Furthermore, in threshing one must take care not to use too much force, lest the useful grain be damaged. Taken as metaphor, this says that when spankings are excessive, either in number or in force, the outcome is likely to be counterproductive.

Robert Larzelere also contributes to this discussion by citing, in a 1993 article in the *Journal of Psychology and*

Theology (Vol. 21, No. 2), two passages in Proverbs which, when considered together, seem to imply that parents should put more emphasis on verbal correction than on spanking, especially as a child advances in years. Proverbs 17:10 says "A rebuke goes deeper into one who has understanding / Than a hundred blows into a fool." Proverbs 22:15 then tells parents that "Foolishness is bound up in the heart of a child; / The rod of discipline will remove it far from him." Larzelere suggests that these two passages can be interpreted to mean spankings are optimally useful with young children who are limited with respect to verbal skills, but beyond age six or seven, as verbal abilities become more sophisticated, spankings become less and less appropriate. This is consistent with research (including Larzelere's own) indicating that spankings are most effective with children between ages two and six.

In the Bible, parents are told that children require strict, consistent discipline in order to develop strength of character. The most familiar of biblical passages concerning child rearing—Proverbs 22:6—makes no mention whatsoever of rods: "Train up a child in the way he should go; / Even when he is old he will not depart from it." The idea that "the child is father of the man" is the heart of the Bible's blueprint for child rearing. Throughout the Bible, parents are urged to make judicious use of a variety of means—guidance, example, explanation, reprimand, restriction, and yes, spanking—to train children in the way they should go such that, as adults, they possess strong character and proper moral bent.

Unfortunately, some conservative Christian spokespersons emphasize spanking in a way that is inflamatory and definitely disproportionate to any biblical reference. Several years ago, for example, I listened to a well-known evangelical minister deliver a sermon on discipline (since I will take certain of this gentleman's remarks out of context—which I definitely did *not* do with Murray Straus—I feel it would be unfair to identify him) in which he made repeated references to the need for parents to express ample affection toward their children, to love their children unconditionally, and to discipline firmly and consistently. Excellent advice.

When it came to spanking, however, he recommended that parents apply a "rod" of choice—a belt, paddle, or switch—"severely," such that the event is never forgotten by the child. He further said parents should not abide a child either refusing to cry or crying excessively in response to a spanking. In the first case, he advised parents to continue spanking until the child was crying suitably. In the second, he again advised that the spanking continue until the child is crying softly, indicating true repentance. When the child displays a "submissive spirit," parents should show affection, reassuring him of their love.

At some point, this begins to sound more like a *thrashing* than a spanking. In fact, although I do not fault this minister's intentions, I would have to say that any parent who took his advice to the extremes he recommends would be guilty of abuse. Fortunately, this gentleman's counsel concerning spanking is not followed by the majority of Christians. It is *not*, as far as I can tell, followed by even the majority of conservative Christians. It does, however, epitomize the other extreme in the spanking debate, one that is no less faulted and troublesome than its legalistic opposite.

PART THREE: COMMON SENSE

The commonsensical view holds that there is a distinction between a spanking and a beating and that the difference can be quantified. Spankings are not abusive; beatings are. An adequate body of law pertaining to the abuse of children already exists. What's needed is not more law, but better enforcement and education. I hope that this book will contribute significantly to the latter.

At best, a spanking is nothing more, nothing less, than a relatively dramatic form of nonverbal communication. It's one means of getting the attention of a child who needs to give that attention quickly; of terminating a behavior that is rapidly escalating out of control; of putting an exclamation point in front of a message the child needs to hear.

Jews use the Yiddish phrase *potch en tuckus* to refer to this sort of benign pop on the buttocks. A scholarly Jewish friend of mine tells me a *potch* (which the *Dictionary of American Slang* defines as a "light spanking") to the child's *tuckus* was for the purpose of "getting the child to pay attention, of bringing the child back to reality." In the Old Country, my friend tells me, a Jewish parent usually coupled the *potch* with nothing more than a stern look, one that said more than a thousand words. "Parents who gave more than a *potch* or two were looked upon as having lost control of both themselves and their children." So a potch was not for the purpose of *establishing* parental authority; indeed, it was only effective if parental authority had already been established. Rather, the *potch* was a *reminder* of parental authority—a mild shock to the *tuckus* that promoted an instantaneous termination of misbehavior and restoration of self-control.

As was the case with the *potch en tuckus*, a spontaneous (as in: without warning) spank to the child's rear end says "Stop!" and "Now hear this!" Having terminated the behavior in question—a tantrum, for instance—and having secured the child's attention, it is necessary that the parent follow through with a consequence of one sort or another. The spank is merely the prelude to the consequence. In the final analysis, the spank is, therefore, *inconsequential*. The follow-through is what's important. Without proper follow-through a spanking is, at the very least, stupid.

The parent might send the child to his/her room for a time, or take away a privilege for the remainder of the day, or simply give the child a stern reprimand. For the most part, and for the purposes of this discussion, the form the consequence takes is fairly arbitrary. All-important is that the spanking not be the consequence, the end in itself. When spankings are administered as if they were an end in and of themselves, parents tend, out of frustration, to overuse them and edge ever closer to abuse.

But make no mistake about it, a properly administered spanking is no more abusive than banishing a child to his room. It would, however, be abusive to keep a child locked in his room for several days. Likewise, a reprimand, in and of itself, is not abusive. But it would be abusive to—in the course of a verbal reprimand—call a child a "little sh-t." In other words, child abuse is not a matter of what *kind* of discipline a parent employs, but the *manner* in which it is delivered.

The term *corporal punishment* is part of the problem one encounters when attempting a general discussion of spanking, because a properly administered spanking is not, strictly speaking, a punishment. Nor, for that matter, is a wrongly administered spanking. According to the scientific definition, a punishment is *a consequence that lessens the likelihood of the behavior with which it is associated.* People who think they can spank certain behaviors out of existence are going to discover otherwise. It has not been my experience or observation that spankings alone, however delivered, will eliminate undesirable behaviors. Parents who believe otherwise will only become increasingly frustrated at the stubborn persistence of their children's misbehavior, and their frustration will drive them to spank more often and harder. Now we're talking about an escalating, "have you learned your lesson yet?" sequence of events. The child, learning nothing of value, will continue making the same or similar mistakes over and over again as the parents, not having learned *their* lesson either, continue harping on the child's rear end.

Parents who cause their children pain usually feel guilty

afterward. Typically, a guilty-feeling parent does something equally foolish to compensate for his mistakes. He might, for instance, suspend enforcement of a certain rule. The child interprets this to mean that *all* rules are suspended. (Children tend to think in terms of black or white—in this case, either there *are* rules or there are not.) So, the child begins to misbehave. By the time the parent acts to reestablish control, things are really out of hand. Before long, the child is on the receiving end of another spanking, and, once again, the parent feels guilty. Second verse, same as the first.

Unless they realize the futility of their approach, these folks are likely, at some point, to beat their kids. It's important to understand, however, that these are not necessarily abusive people. More often than not, these are people who want to do right by their children. The proper intervention here is education (offered, as opposed to imposed), not more legislation.

Whenever I was asked by the courts or a social services agency to counsel parents who had beaten their children, I did not waste time attempting to persuade them to stop spanking altogether. Instead of trying to paddle back up the stream of their upbringing and their value system, I advised them on how to spank *strategically;* as in occasionally, conservatively, and only to secure the child's attention. My experience is that this approach is far more fruitful than one which holds that these folks cannot be trusted to spank appropriately. This tack is also more in keeping with the finding that parents who do not give themselves permission to spank, even lightly, are more apt to explode toward their children. My work with previously abusive parents also reinforces my belief that education, not further legislation, is the solution to whatever problems attend the general issue of spanking.

In short, it is possible to spank a child *well*, to do it *right* and make it *work*. The problem with spanking is that many, if not most, parents make a sorry mess of it.

The typical spanking scenario begins with a child doing something that is clearly out of bounds, as in leaping from a coffee table onto a sofa. The child's parents react by jabbering, bobbing up and down at the waist, and flapping their arms. The child notices that despite their agitated manner, they have done absolutely nothing. He files this valuable information away in a neuron bank marked "High Priority."

Fifteen minutes later (if not sooner), he again climbs up on the coffee table and propels himself onto the sofa. His parents jabber, bob, and flap as before. And again nothing of consequence happens. Remarkable! So, the child climbs and leaps again. This time, before his parents stop flapping, one of them says, "If you do that again, I'll have to spank you! Do you understand!?"

Of course he understands. He knows a challenge when he sees one. His parents, meanwhile, are becoming increasingly frustrated over his "disobedience" or "stubbornness" or whatever term they use to describe what's happening. Five more times he leaps, and five more times his parents bob, flap, and threaten. On the ninth leap, he knocks over a lamp and his parents descend on him like furies, flapping their hands against his rear end, shouting, "We told you not to leap, and look what you did!" The child shrieks and twists, trying unsuccessfully to avoid his fate.

For several hours following the incident, the home is wrapped in a mantle of gloom. No one talks; no one laughs. The child feels cheated. The parents feel guilty. All in all, the entire incident has been a waste of time, energy, and a lamp.

But it wasn't the decision to spank that was wrong. It was the *timing* of the decision and way it was carried out. You see, in spanking as in comedy, timing and delivery are everything. In the chapter that follows, the reader will learn the dos and don'ts of both.

Chapter Two

The Sound of One Hand Clapping

It's almost inevitable that at my speaking engagements someone will ask if I *believe* in spanking. I've always felt this was a peculiar way of asking the question, as if spanking were a doctrine or principle of child rearing rather than a selective disciplinary act. Using the word *believe* in conjunction with spanking also suggests that a parent's entire attitude toward and approach to the rearing of children can be summed up in terms of whether or not the parent spanks. Indeed, as we have seen, there are those who think that is precisely the case. The form of the question also reflects the controversy that presently surrounds this subject, a controversy that is absurdly disproportionate to the actual significance of swatting a child's rear end and yet which begs close examination because of its far-reaching political and cultural implications.

In any case, to say that I *believe* in spanking children implies that spankings are in some way essential to their proper upbringing. I do *not* hold that opinion; therefore, I do not *believe* in spanking. On the other hand, I spanked both of our children on occasion, and while this decision did not always produce the desired outcome, I have no regrets about doing so.

It was never in my plans to spank. I simply did it when I was so moved. In general, I spanked when one of them was blatantly disrespectful, flagrantly disobedient, outspokenly defiant, extremely rude or insensitive, or in the early throes of a tantrum. But I did not spank on all such occasions. Only sometimes. Selectively. When I felt like it. There was no science to my method, no calculation, psychology, or forethought. When I spanked, it was spontaneous, like the proverbial bolt out of the blue. But don't get me wrong. My spankings were definitely not impulsive, emotionally driven acts. I was in control, always, *using* my temper rather than *losing* it. A swat on the rear end from Daddy was a sudden, forceful—but not especially painful, if at all—indication to the child in question that I was *in* control, not out of it. I spanked not because I had become upended by the child's behavior, but to demonstrate that I was *not* upended; not frustrated, but definitely disapproving.

In addition, a spanking communicated my insistence that the child cease and desist the targeted misbehavior *at once;* that he or she "reel it in," so to speak, and immediately so. In that sense, my spankings were *restorative.* They were a communication of authoritative resolve, and a means of helping the child restore self-control. The way I looked at it, the child was "off track" and needed to get back on, quickly.

Children being children, there are times when they careen off on some out-of-control tangent. If children never lost control, they would not need parents. There are times when a child's loss of control can be ignored—as when the child becomes furious at a block tower that keeps falling over—and there are times when, even though the loss of control cannot be ignored, it can be dealt with patiently—as in sending a child to his room until a fit of hysterical laughing has subsided. Those sorts of "misbehaviors" are of minor consequence. They're a simple matter of maturity,

things time will take care of. But then there are misbehaviors that cannot be ignored, that unless "nipped in
the bud" will only get worse. One cannot afford patience
when it comes to disrespect, defiance, tantrums, and antisocial behavior. These must be dealt with swiftly and, more
often than not, dramatically. The child must know that
these behaviors will not, under any circumstances, be tol-
erated, not because they are threatening to the parent, but
because they threaten the child's ultimate *ability to succeed*.
After all, whether the challenge is social, marital, professional, spiritual, political, or economic, true success comes
to those who respect authority as well as their fellow man,
know when and how to obey as well as when and how to
lead, and are in control of themselves. Our children cannot
afford for us to tolerate transgressions that run counter to
these rules of reality. Does this mean that every time a
child is disrespectful, etc., a parent should spank? No, it
definitely does not. It simply means that under those circumstances it is not inappropriate to swat the child's rear
end. But there's more to it than that; much more, in fact,
as we shall soon see.

Before we go any further, however, here's a story involving my daughter, Amy, that will illustrate what I've said
thus far: When Amy was seven or eight, her mother and I
both worked in separate locations outside the home. During this time, we had an understanding that whoever ar-
rived home from work first would cook supper. One day,
having hidden up the street as long as I could, I came home
and began preparing the evening meal. I was standing at
the counter when Amy walked through the kitchen. Over
my shoulder, I said, "Amy, Daddy needs you to set the
table, sweetheart."

She stopped, wheeled around, and adopting the chal-
lenging stance of a streetfighter, said, "No, I won't! I'm
sick and tired of doing everything around here! Eric never
does anything and it's not fair and I'm not setting the table
because I just won't and you can't make me and . . ."

I can only tell you that I felt suddenly *inspired,* for lack of a better term. In the midst of this tirade, I wiped my hands on a towel, calmly crossed the space between us, took Amy's arm with my left hand, turned her to the side, and—right hand accelerating downward—smacked her good and hard on the bottom.

Her eyes and mouth popped wide open as the swat propelled her forward six inches or so. Needless to say, she was rigid with surprise and completely silent.

"Now, hear this!" I barked, my eyes boring into hers, "You will not speak to me in that tone of voice! You will not speak to your mother in that tone of voice! You will not speak to *any* adult in that tone of voice! *Do you understand!!?*"

Her head bobbed rapidly up and down.

"Good! And you will do as you are told in this family!" I was not yelling, mind you, but rather enunciating every word à la Jack Webb in that movie about Marine drill instructors. "So, you *will* set the table! And after you have set the table, you will go to your room and stay there until supper. And after supper, which you may eat with the rest of the family, you will go back to your room, put your pajamas on, and get in bed, because at that point, your day, young lady, is over! Now, git!"

And she got. I later noticed that although the table had been set, my place mat was turned around backward, so that the silverware pointed menacingly at me instead of away from me. Amy has always had a way of making her point. Oh, well.

There you have an illustration of what I mean by a *spanking:* a swat (or perhaps two) swiftly applied to a child's rear end by means of a parent's open hand. The purpose is *not* to cause pain, but to (a) secure the child's immediate, undivided attention, (b) quickly terminate an undesirable behavior, (c) secure control of a situation that threatens to quickly deteriorate, (d) provide a forceful reminder to the child of your authority, or (e) all of the above. In other words, a spanking is nothing more than an occasionally effective form of nonverbal communication.

The effectiveness of a spanking can be maximized by observing the following "Rules of Palm":

• **Be quick about it.** Don't give numerous threats or warnings (although one—and only one—warning might be warranted under certain circumstances), or build up to a spanking in any other equally unnecessary, waste-of-everyone's-time manner. Just do it, without ceremony. Especially in cases where a child is rapidly losing control or has just been flagrantly disrespectful toward a parent, a spanking should be like a lightning strike. In the midst of a sudden storm of misbehavior, *ka-boom!* The element of surprise all but insures that the misbehavior in question will be brought to an abrupt halt and that the child will be focused intently, expectantly, upon you, at which point you can deliver your "Now hear this!" message and, if warranted, a truly effective consequence. A colleague of mine tells me that if one of his children did not immediately comply with an instruction, he would count to three, with the intention of spanking at that point if the child was still obstinate. That warning was sufficient to prevent escalation of either the child's noncompliance or his level of frustration. Although I never counted, my friend's technique sounds very reasonable to me, and is certainly consistent with my viewpoint.

• **Do not ever spank as a "last resort."** In other words, don't allow a child's misbehavior to escalate before delivering a spanking. When a spanking seems called for, spank. Don't threaten, talk yourself blue in the face, or equivocate. Nip the misbehavior in the proverbial "bud." When it comes to a spanking, in hesitation, all is lost. Furthermore, if you wait until you're at the "end of your rope" before you spank, you are only teaching your child how to pull your rope. Most parents make the mistake of giving one warning after another in the face of a child's misbehavior, accumulating more and more frustration in the process. Finally, unable to contain their frustration any longer, they explode. And unload. Instead of *whack!* or *whack whack!*, it's *whack whack whack whack whack whack whack whack whack whack whack!* In the aftermath of this cataclysm, the parent feels guilty and the child feels resentful. Meanwhile, absolutely nothing has been accomplished. Furthermore, a history of that sort is destined to repeat itself.

One reason parents tend to view spankings as a last resort measure, something to be used when all else has failed, is because spanking has taken on so many negative overtones. It's come to be regarded as something akin to fighting fire with fire—responding to one bad thing with something equally bad. From this point of view, spanking is a regrettable something you only do when a child will not listen to reason. Well, I have news: *Young children don't listen to reason.* Reasoning is something older children and adults are able to do. Young children are bundles of impulses which burst forth at the damnedest of times. So you can forget reason and cut directly to the chase. When a young child loses control, parents must secure control. Again, I'm not saying that each and every time a child loses control, a parent should spank. In fact, spankings quickly lose their effectiveness if they are daily fare. I'm saying that if the situation seems appropriate for a spanking, and you feel so inclined, then stand and deliver! As soon as the child begins to lose control or commits an outrageous act (e.g., spitting at an adult), *whack!* Now hear this! Nor am I saying that words are unnecessary. As you will soon see, words are *absolutely* necessary. I'm simply saying that you cannot *reason* a child out of disrespect, defiance, tantrums, or other antisocial behaviors. These are things that must be stopped. When the child is old enough to understand why you would not allow these snowballs to roll downhill, he or she will understand. Words won't do it, time will.

• **Spank in anger (but never, ever in a rage).** You heard me correctly, but I want you to read this section very, very carefully so that you don't misunderstand my meaning. Here, I am using *anger* in its original, biblical sense. In the Old Testament, when God is referred to as being angry, He is *not* out of control. Rather, he is putting on a dramatic display of disapproval in order to get mankind's attention. He is making himself perfectly clear, so as to leave no doubt but that He is absolutely serious. Likewise, if you're going to swat a child's rear end, it is right to make it perfectly clear that you disapprove of the child's present behavior. There should be absolutely no doubt in the child's mind but that you are displeased, as in biblically *angry*.

I know, I know, you've always heard that one should *never* spank in anger. I remember, as a child, misbehaving and being told by my stepfather that he could not spank me at the moment because he was angry. He'd send me to my room where I'd wait until he was cool, calm, and collected. He sometimes made me wait for several hours. Regardless, the waiting was psychological torture. The whole time, I'd sit in my room, imagining my fate. With each passing moment, my stepfather's hand grew bigger and bigger, then it sprouted spikes and electrodes through which flowed thousands of volts of electric current. Then I would imagine that he was so calm, so detached when he finally spanked me that he'd forget to stop—that he'd start daydreaming in the middle of beating my butt and just keep going on and on, oblivious to my screams of torment.

By the time he finally came to my room to administer justice, I was a blithering idiot. I'd fall to the floor, prostrate, begging and pleading for mercy.

"I've learned my lesson!" I'd wail. "I'll never do it again! I promise. Oh, please, please, please, don't spank me. I'll wash your car every day this week. Give me your shoes! I'll shine them! I'll go to work for you tomorrow! You can stay home! No one will notice! Oh, please, please, please, please, please!"

"I'm sorry," he'd say, with this rueful tone, "but I have no choice."

No choice? Well then let me talk to the guy who's making you do this, for Pete's sake!

After this little deterioration into schizophrenia, he'd tell me the spanking was going to hurt *him* more than it hurt *me*.

"Then don't do it!" I'd yell. "I don't want you to hurt yourself!"

At this point, I'd usually feel a warm gush of liquid down my left pantleg.

"What's that smell?" he'd snarl. Then, seeing what was happening, he'd go completely bonkers, turn me over his knee and do what he should have done three hours before. At this point, I'm so relieved that it's finally happening that I release the entire contents of my bladder in his lap, which prompts him to further fury. Nonetheless, I am left with a meager sense of satisfaction, of revenge.

All this transpired, mind you, simply because my step-father would not spank when he was angry. Needless to say, by the time the spanking was over, I felt no remorse concerning my misdeed, only resentment. I clearly remember, after these incidents, planning my eventual revenge. It might be useful to mention, in this context, that I am not now, nor have I ever been, a violent person. Although the manner in which my stepfather spanked—and he felt that spanking was the best answer to just about any misbe-havior—was certainly violent, both physically and psycho-logically, violence is simply not part of my makeup. I never got my revenge—the whole idea seems supremely foolish to me in retrospect—nor have I ever "displaced" my anger toward any other living thing. (I realize, however, that ra-bid antispankers will view the fact that I was spanked as a child and, later, spanked my own children as "proof" that violence breeds violence—that I did, indeed, displace my rage, concerning which I am simply "in denial." Don't you just love psychobabble?)

Please understand that I recommend spanking in anger only in the context of spanking a child before the child's misbehavior begins to escalate. If you do not spank fairly quickly, you are likely to be in a rage by the time you apply hand to butt. You will whack whack whack whack whack and feel guilt guilt guilt guilt guilt. The further reason for spanking in anger is because the child on the receiving end should definitely understand, feel, your disapproval. A sudden, swift swat to the rear should say, in effect, "I will not tolerate what you are doing!" You cannot effectively communicate intolerance if you are either in a rage or, as was the case with my stepfather, calm and composed. There must be a *force* of emotion, determination, and purpose behind the communication. Once you have secured the child's attention, the child should see, written all over your face, that you mean business.

• **Use your hand, and your hand only.** As I said before, the idea is *not* to cause pain, but to communicate. In the second place, your hand says, in a way that belts, switches, and paddles do not, that it's *you* talking. In the third, by using your hand, you know when to stop (just in case you need a reminder).

I have always felt that a spanking is an *intimate* act, one that requires an intimate relationship in order to be absorbed effectively. The hand is intimate, personal. A belt is not. A belt puts distance between the parent and the act. I've heard people say that a parent's hands are for loving, not for punishing, and that a child will become confused if a parent's hands serve both purposes. More often than not, these same folks will refer to scriptural mention of the "rod" in conjunction with the discipline of children. As I've already discussed in the previous chapter, I'm convinced that the "rod" of the Old Testament was not necessarily a stick of one sort or another. I prefer to believe that "rod" is a figurative reference to parental authority. Just as the shepherd's rod, or staff, was not for beating the flock, but for guiding it, the "rod" of parenthood is a call for the proper exercise of authority.

Besides, belts, switches, and "rods" of other description cannot possibly be used without causing a certain amount of pain. I can only hope that by this point the reader is sufficiently convinced that spankings do not need to hurt in order to be effective. I hope, in fact, to have convinced you that beyond a very temporary and quickly subsiding sting, the most effective spankings do not cause any significant pain at all. That isn't the point. Shock, yes. Pain, as in lingering physical hurt, no.

In answer to those who claim that using the hand to spank causes the child to fear the parent's hand and, therefore, the parent, I can only say that this might well be the outcome of spankings with the hand if the parent's intent *is* to cause pain. But if the intent is simply—as I can't say enough—to terminate an undesirable behavior and focus the child's attention on the parent, then I fail to see how the parent's hand can become an object of fear. All of these myths concerning use of the hand grow out of the idea that in order to be effective, spankings must be painful.

My conclusions in this regard are based, in part, on personal evidence. I never spanked either of my children with anything other than my hand, yet neither child ever acted generally fearful of me. They never shrank away from me if I lifted my hand to scratch the side of my nose, nor did they cower if I reached out to embrace them or give them a fatherly pat.

In preparation for the writing of this book, I asked scores of people around the country questions concerning their experiences of having been spanked as children. The only people who told me that they felt their parents' spankings had been abusive were those whose parents had either (a) spanked with something other than their hands and/or (b) struck them in places other than on the buttocks. Surprisingly enough, however, most of the people who felt abused in these ways as children did not bear any resentment toward their parents as adults. As one woman, whose father had beaten her on numerous occasions with a belt, told me, "I don't have any hard feelings toward him for it. After all, he was only doing what most parents of his generation felt was perfectly acceptable, even necessary. His sin was ignorance."

Last, but not least, to those who justify using belts, paddles, or whatever by saying, in effect, "the Bible says to do it that way," I would simply point out that the Old Testament also says that men should wear tassles on the hems of their garments. Are these people being selective, or what? They'll hit their kids with belts, but I'll just bet they wouldn't be caught dead in public wearing multicolored robes with tassled hems.

• **Apply the hand to the child's rear end only.** God obviously designed this area to absorb impact. It is completely unnecessary, by the way, to pull down the child's clothing before administering the swat. Again—and I cannot emphasize this enough—the purpose is not pain. If you're not out to cause pain, and you want to catch the child by surprise, then you don't need to remove the child's clothing. (Furthermore, removing a child's clothing before a spanking introduces a thoroughly inappropriate element of humiliation into the process.)

Despite the unnecessary amount of ritual that generally attended a spanking by my stepfather, there were occasional times when, to get my attention, he'd simply place his left hand, palm out, alongside my buttocks, and slap his left hand with his right hand. The resulting *clap!* was always enough to jolt me into paying attention. Just a reminder. If that appeals to you more than actually swatting a child's rear end, go ahead and give it a try.

• **Follow through with a clear, stern message and, if need be, a restrictive consequence of one sort or another.** In the story about Amy and setting the table, my swat to her rear end was neither the message nor the consequence. In accord with my philosophy of spanking, I

swatted her butt to bring an abrupt halt to her disrespectful tirade, focus her attention upon me, and remind her of
my authority. Having accomplished all three objectives, I
sent her a strong message, repeated my instruction to her
in no uncertain terms and tone, and directed her to her
room for the remainder of the evening, which was consid-
erably shortened by an early bedtime.

The message should be short, to the point, and delivered in a stern, commanding tone. Do your best to keep it
to twenty-five words or less. The longer it is, the more you
go on and on, the less clear you will be and the more likely
it is you will lose the child's attention.

If we're talking about a toddler, then it's probably best
to get down to the child's level, take the child by the shoulders, and use no more than ten words, as in, "No! I will
not let you spit at me!"

Consequences are a problem with toddlers because their
memories are so short. If you send a two-year-old to his
room for ten minutes, by the time the ten minutes have
elapsed, the child will probably not be able to remember
why he was sent into exile. Trying to make a two-year-old
sit in time-out is equally problematic because it's the rare
toddler that will sit for longer than a few seconds. Holding
this age child in the chair will probably send him into a
rage and will set the stage for ongoing power struggles.
With all this in mind, I generally recommend that once the
ten-words-or-less message has been delivered, the parent
pick the child up, carry him to the nearest chair, and set
him in it with the words, "You will sit here until I tell you
to get up!" Then, the parent should take one, maybe two
steps back and say, "Get up." At this point, the parent
should simply walk away.

In so doing, the parent has accomplished all that needs
to be accomplished with this age child—all that possibly
can be accomplished, in most cases. The parent has:
• demonstrated that he or she can move the child, but the
child cannot move the parent;

• acted assertively, but not aggressively;
• demonstrated his or her complete control over the situation.

All of the above amounts to a clear, competent show of authority, which is all that's necessary. Futhermore, let's face it, if the parent doesn't immediately tell the child to get up, the child's going to get up anyway. Ah, but in this case, the child isn't rebelling by getting up—he's cooperating! He's doing what he's been told to do!

Let's review that whole situation, so you can see how quickly it's over and done with: The encounter begins with the child spitting at, let's say, his mother, perhaps because she has refused to give him a cookie. She turns her most uncivilized little one immediately to the side and with moderate force, whacks his rear end twice. She then gets down to his level, takes him by the shoulders, and brings him face-to-face.

"No!" she says, in a stern, commanding tone. "You will not spit at me!"

She picks him up, carries him to the nearest chair, sets him down, and, still holding him under the arms, says, "You sit here until I tell you to get up!" She releases him, takes one step back, and says, "Get up." Then, she turns and walks away. The whole encounter takes no longer than ten seconds. Over and done with. Short and sweet. And the child is, let me assure you, *impressed.*

With a child older than three, the message can be slightly longer, it can be delivered from a standing position, and the restrictive consequence can be of longer duration. The child can be banished to his or her room for a period of time. A privilege—going outside, having a friend over to play, watching television—can be taken away for the remainder of the day. The child can be sent to bed early. Or, a combination of the above. In some cases, however, the message can stand on its own and be the end of it. It's not, in other words, always necessary to impose a restriction or take away a privilege. Sometimes, a forceful

message of disapproval is sufficient. Anything more might be overkill.

In some situations, it might be impossible to impose a consequence, in which case the pop on the rear and the message will have to do. Once, when Eric, our firstborn, was three, we were at a friend's house and Eric was absorbed with something novel our host had provided as a plaything. When it was time to leave, Eric became stubborn. He wasn't ready to leave, he told us. It was time to leave, we said. "No!" he countered, "I'm not leaving!"

Without a moment's hesitation, I reached down, hauled him to his feet, walked him into the front hallway where we were alone, swatted him on the bottom, and said, "Yes, Eric, we're leaving. You are going to thank Mrs. Johnson for letting you play with the puzzle [or whatever it was], take my hand, and walk with me to the car. Got it?"

Wide-eyed, he nodded his head.

"Good." I led him back into the living room, where he said his thanks, and we left. It was over and done with in a heartbeat and no more was said. By the time we got home, it was pointless to do anything more, so the incident was "forgotten." Had we been at our next-door neighbor's house, however, I might have led him home and sent him to his room for an hour or so.

Sometimes, an apology might be the consequence. On one occasion, when Amy, our second (and last) child, was four or five, she was playing with a friend in our front yard. I was sitting on the porch watching them when suddenly, the friend tripped and fell, face down, in the grass. Amy thought this was hilarious. As Amy stood by laughing, I picked up her little friend and made sure she was okay. Amy continued to split her sides as I cleaned dirt from her friend's face and grass from her mouth. I then took Amy and led her inside, indicating to her playmate that we would return in a moment.

As soon as we were inside, and without warning, I swatted Amy's backside. Needless to say, her laughing ceased. I

turned her so we were face-to-face and said, "When someone hurts themselves, it's mean to laugh. You're going to
go outside and tell Shelly that you're sorry and make sure
she's all right. Do you understand?"

"Yes, Daddy. I'm sorry."

"Don't tell me, tell Shelly. Go!"

And outside she went, where she made her apologies,
and the play resumed.

My point is that in the final analysis, the age of the child
and the particulars of the situation will dictate what you
can and cannot do. Sometimes consequences are possible,
sometimes they're not. Sometimes an apology is all that's
necessary. Regardless, you should always, always, send a
clear, stern message of disapproval and direction.

• **Spank only in private, never in public.** Just as it is
usually embarrassing for a parent to have a child act up in
public, so it is humiliating for a child to be spanked in public. As I've already said, a spanking is an intimate act, one
that requires an already-existing intimate relationship in
order to be effective. As such, it should also be done in an
intimate manner. Privately, not publicly.

Note that when Eric refused to leave our friend's house,
I did not pop his behind in front of our host. Out of respect not only for Eric, but our host as well, I removed him
to the front hallway. Did our friend know what I was doing? Of course, but that isn't the point. The point is that
Eric and I were alone. Think about it. If I'd spanked Eric
in front of our host, Eric would have been acutely aware of
our host's presence and, as a result, he would not have been
focusing exclusively on me. My message, therefore, would
have had less impact. Later, when he reviewed the situation, foremost in his mind would have been the fact that
our host witnessed the spanking. By removing him to a
private place, I insured that his memory would not have
been thus "polluted."

Likewise, when Amy laughed at her friend's misfortune,
I took her into the house. Spanking her in front of her

friend would have been humiliating. As a result, Amy might have blamed the spanking on her friend, in which case her apology would have been hollow. I wanted Amy to take complete responsibility for her behavior as well as the consequence. Therefore, I popped her behind in private.

In Eric's case, our host was not involved in his spanking. In Amy's, her friend was not involved. There were no distractions in either situation. In both cases, it was just me and the child. The spankings, therefore, were intimate. The children were better able, therefore, to focus on me. They heard me more clearly. In every sense of the term, therefore, because the spankings were conducted in private, they had more "impact."

• **Spank only occasionally.** In order to have the desired dramatic effect, a spanking must not be too predictable. The more often a child is spanked, the less dramatic any given spanking will be. Fact is, children who are spanked a lot develop an "immunity" to spankings. They develop a "so what?" attitude toward them. How much is too much? The answer depends on the age of the child. With a toddler, more than once a week is probably too much. With a four- or five-year-old, once a month is a good benchmark. With a child six and older, you reach the point of diminishing returns at one spanking every three months or so. And, by the way, by the time a child is nine or ten, spankings should cease entirely. If you don't have a child's respect and attention by then, no amount of slapping the child's rear end is going to matter.

Parents who spank a lot generally do so because they believe spankings are in and of themselves *corrective*—that the pain of a spanking will persuade the child never to misbehave in that particular fashion again. The evidence to the contrary is overwhelming. Children who are spanked a lot do not stop misbehaving. They misbehave not only more and more, but also more and more cleverly. In other words, they learn how to get away with misbehavior. Eventually, getting away with misbehavior becomes a game and they begin setting bigger and bigger goals for themselves. What can I get away with next? becomes the dominant challenge in their lives. Meanwhile, their parents spank more and more, with less and less effect. Finally, the parents give up, saying, "I can't do a thing with him." And they're absolutely right! Now, unfortunately, it's society's turn, and society has never done as good a job as parents could have done in the first place. When it comes to spanking, less is definitely more.

In closing, let me remind the reader that I am not recommending spankings. There's always more than one way to skin the proverbial cat. In that sense, antispankers are absolutely correct—there are always alternatives to spanking. The question, however, becomes: In any given situation, is the alternative as effective as a spanking would have been? After having assisted in the rearing of two children and twenty-two years of working with families, I've reached the conclusion that there are times when a quick spank to the rear of a child is worth more than a thousand words. The spanking serves as a *catalyst,* a *spice* that enhances the child's "taste" of his or her parent's authority, the message, and the consequence.

I'm not one to say that you should or shouldn't spank. I'm simply saying that if you choose to do so, please, for your child's sake, do it properly.

Chapter Three

Questions?

Q. Was it Dr. Spock, with his permissive philosophy, who set the antispanking movement in motion?

A. Hardly. Actually, the notion that Spock advocated a permissive approach to child rearing is largely myth. His approach was child-centered in the sense that he placed significant emphasis on the developmental needs of the child, but for the most part his advice was grounded in tradition. Spock was definitely *not* in favor of letting the child dictate the course and circumstances of his or her upbringing. The myth of Spock's supposed permissiveness got its start in the late '60s, during which he became an outspoken critic of America's involvement in the Vietnam War. The Nixon administration, seeking to discredit the antiwar movement, accused Spock of having encouraged parents to raise children such that they had no respect for authority. Hogwash! In truth, Spock was fairly old-fashioned when it came to specific parenting advice. Furthermore, the better part of his *Common Sense Book of Baby and Child Care,* first published in 1946, concerned medical issues, such as how to tell the difference between roseola and the measles, what to do if a child develops a fever, etc. Throughout, Spock reassures parents and gives them permission to follow their intutions.

The second edition of his book was published in 1968, at the height of his antiwar activism. Even though many child-rearing "experts" were taking an unequivocal no-spanking stance, Spock's advice concerning spanking continued to be fairly neutral. He writes:

> If an angry parent keeps himself from spanking, he may show his irritation in other ways: for instance, by nagging the child half the day, or trying to make him feel deeply guilty. I'm not particularly advocating spanking, but I think it is less poisonous than lengthy disapproval, because it clears the air, for parent and child.

The first child-rearing authority to tell parents, in no uncertain terms, *not* to spank was Selma Fraiberg, author of the *The Magic Years,* which has sold nearly a million copies since its publication in 1959. Fraiberg warned that spankings caused children to fear their parents and simply become more clever and deceptive concerning the pursuit of mischief. In 1994, the antispanking movement continues to echo Fraiberg's emphasis on the supposedly negative psychological effects of spankings.

The antispanking position was elaborated upon in the two most popular parenting books of the '70s, *Parent Effectiveness Training* (1970) by psychologist Thomas Gordon and *Your Child's Self-Esteem* (1970) by family counselor Dorothy Briggs. Both Gordon and Briggs advocate a democratic approach to child rearing which presumes that parent and child are equals. Gordon defines authoritarian parents as those who believe they have a "right to exercise authority or power" over their children. These parents, he says, employ essentially the same "obedience training" techniques used by animal trainers, including the use of physical pain to promote compliance. As a result, writes Gordon:

> Children often become cowed, fearful, and nervous . . . often turn on their trainers with hostility and vengeance; and often break down physically or emotionally under the stress of trying to learn behavior that is either difficult or unpleasant for them (169–170).

Briggs is equally adamant, not to mention apocalyptic, when it comes to spankings. Her warning concerning the effects of spanking is almost word-for-word what we hear from today's spokespersons for the antispanking movement:

> . . . every spanking fills a child with negative feelings that may be translated into further misbehavior. . . . Spanking does not teach inner conviction. It teaches fear, deviousness, lying, and aggression. No matter how we slice it, spanking is a physical assault of a bigger person on a smaller one. And yet we tell children they shouldn't hit someone smaller or weaker. We can all smile at the apparent contradiction of the mother who slaps her child, saying, "I'll teach you not to hit!" Yet, studies show that youngsters subjected to overt parental aggression are far more likely to be physically aggressive and hostile in their relations with others (234).

Here, Briggs provides the antispanking movement with one of its primary themes: a spanking is, in effect, indistinguishable from any other physical assault on the part of a parent toward a child. To my knowledge, this was the first time a parenting authority of significant stature leaned toward actually defining spanking as child abuse.

Q. Should teachers be allowed to spank?

A. Spankings have absolutely no place in a school, public or private. Unless they take place in the context of a trusting, loving relationship, spankings will not be effective. In most cases, the only two people who have this kind of a relationship with a child are his or her parents. They are, therefore, the only people who have any business laying an open hand to the child's rear end. Without intimacy, a spanking is nothing more than an act of hit and run.

A spanking properly administered by a parent is an act of authority, but a spanking administered by a teacher is an act of desperation. In and of itself, it says the teacher has failed to adequately establish control of the classroom. Teachers themselves admit to this failure when they justify spanking students by saying (as they *always* do) that spankings are a "last resort." A teacher who spanks runs the risk of instilling not respect, but disrespect; not willingness to comply, but resentment and determination to get even. These are the outcomes when a history of nurturance and trust are missing from the relationship between spanker and spankee.

Teachers have told me "there are some children who can only be reached by spanking them." Yet it's inevitable that other teachers manage to "reach" these same children without ever spanking them. An in-school paddling, therefore, says more about the person behind the paddle than it does the student. Quite simply, it says the teacher has no business teaching.

Granted, discipline in schools is more of a problem today than it was thirty or forty years ago. But the paddle is not going to restore it. Discipline will be restored to the classroom when high standards for teachers are restored and, in so doing, dignity to the profession of teaching; when high academic standards are restored, thus enhancing the seriousness of the educational process in the eyes of students; and most importantly, when parents of misbehaving children get their priorities in order and instead of defending their children when they misbehave in school, get solidly behind teachers and hold their children strictly accountable for their classroom behavior.

Q. **As a teacher, I think your position on corporal punishment in schools only shows how little you know about the problems of teaching. You obviously don't realize, for example, that many teachers have more of a loving relationship with some of their students than do the parents of those students. In cases such as these, what do you have to say about a teacher spanking a child?**

A. I am quite aware that a teacher may sometimes have a more affectionate relationship with a certain child than do the child's parents. In that case, neither the teacher *nor* the child's parents have any business spanking the child.

Q. Why is the follow-through so important and what are some ways of accomplishing it?

A. A spanking is fairly worthless without a suitable follow-through. In other words, a spanking alone is not disciplinary in the sense that it does not *teach* a child anything. The teaching, the discipline, comes *after* the spanking. The follow-through should be delivered immediately and decisively, meaning calmly yet in no uncertain terms. It must be perfectly clear to the child that you are disapproving of his behavior, if not angry—*using* your temper as opposed to losing it. The nature and extent of the follow-through will depend largely on the age of the child. In some cases, a few words of reprimand may be sufficient to put the child back on track. If you feel that a more demonstrative follow-through is necessary—and you should by all means go with your intuition—then:

• Take away an important privilege, such as going outside, for the remainder of the day. (With a two-year-old or a young three-year-old, removing a privilege for an hour or so will probably suffice.)

• Require that the child apologize to the offended party.

• Banish the child to his room for an extended period of time, perhaps the remainder of the day. (Again, this is too long for a child younger than, say, forty-two months, in which case an hour or so is enough.)

• Send the child to bed early.

• Require that the child write the same sentence (e.g., "In the future, I will not scream when my parents tell me to do something.") twenty-five or more times.

• Confine the child to an isolated, boring area of the home (e.g., the downstairs, or guest bathroom, an alcove, the back hallway) for three minutes to thirty minutes. (The older the child, the longer the time. Periods longer than thirty minutes should be spent in the child's room.) This is known as "time-out."

. Combine two or more of the above as you see fit.

You don't have to be consistent in your choice of follow-through, but you must, by all means, be consistent about following through. To explain: Let's just say that in the course of a month your six-year-old reacts defiantly to you on three separate occasions. Each time, you pop his rear end. The first time, you follow up with thirty minutes of confinement in the downstairs bathroom. The second time, you confine him to the downstairs bathroom for thirty minutes *and* send his best friend—with whom he was playing at the time of the incident—home. The third time, you banish him to his room for the remainder of the day and put him to bed one hour early. On each occasion, you demonstrate your disapproval—your *intolerance,* no less—in equally effective, yet different ways. The spankings did nothing more than terminate his impertinence and rivet his attention on you, insuring that your message would come across loud and clear.

Q. Ideally, my husband and I would like to follow up on our occasional spankings with ten minutes of time-out in the downstairs bathroom. Our very strong-willed six-year-old, however, will not cooperate. He refuses to go to the bathroom (or anywhere else for that matter), and if we successfully manage to get him there, he keeps coming out. Do you have any suggestions?

A. You've described a problem that's quite commonplace, especially when the child in question is highly disobedient. As you've already discovered, the attempt to enforce time-out with that type of child may create a whole new set of problems, and solve none. For that reason, I generally recommend that time-out be used in conjunction with loss of privileges.

• Make a list of four privileges (freedoms) your son enjoys on a regular, if not daily, basis. These probably include going outside to play, having a friend over, watching television, and staying up until eight-thirty (or his normal bedtime).

• Rank these privileges in order of their importance to your son. Most children attach greatest value to going outside, but that can vary. In any case, staying up until normal bedtime should be last on the list, even if that doesn't accurately represent its value.

• Post this list on the refrigerator.

• Make a second list of the five most troublesome of your son's misbehaviors, as in: Saying "no!" when you tell him to do something, ignoring you when you tell him to do something, calling you names when you refuse a request, teasing the dog, and bouncing on the sofa.

• After going over this list of "target behaviors" with your son, post it on the refrigerator as well, next to the first list.

• Now, whenever a target behavior (or a behavior closely similar to a target behavior) occurs, instruct your son that since he's done something that's on his list, he must go to time-out for ten minutes. But, tell him that if he'd rather not spend ten minutes in the bathroom, he can choose to lose a privilege instead. If he chooses the latter, then he gives up the privilege of going outside to play (or the most valuable privilege on the list) for the remainder of the day. The next time he chooses loss of privilege over time-out, he loses the next most valuable privilege for the remainder of the day, and so on.

• If he initially agrees to time-out, but becomes uncooperative on the way to the bathroom, simply take away a privilege instead. Likewise, if he comes out of time-out before his ten minutes are up, take away a privilege. Always take the most valuable privilege first, and work your way down the list from there. Privileges lost (or given up) are lost for the remainder of that day only. Your son should always begin every new day with all of his freedoms intact.

This combination of follow-throughs will take you out of the power struggle over time-out. It's easy to see that in most cases a child would rather cooperate with ten minutes of time-out than lose a privilege for the remainder of the day. This is an example of what I term the "Godfather Principle" in that you'll be making your son an offer he can't refuse.

Q. Our two-year-old has recently decided to become truly "terrible." My husband believes he's old enough for a spanking every now and then, but I'm not so sure. What's your opinion?

A. If a child is old enough to defy you, then he's old enough to be spanked, and I seem to recall that two-year-olds can be fairly defiant. That doesn't mean twos *should* be spanked, mind you, but that they *can* be, if their parents are so inclined and understand how to do so effectively.

I am, however, *completely opposed* to the practice of slapping a toddler on the back of his hand for touching something off limits. This rule applies even if he is reaching for something hot. If parents have time to slap, they also have time to grab the child's hand and pull it away with a sharp "No!" At this point, and depending on the child's verbal skills, the parent should either distract or, having secured the child's attention, briefly explain why the child should keep his distance from the item in question.

During the toddler stage, at which time a child's exploratory urges peak, it is best and most economical—in terms of time, energy, and money—simply to put tempting objects out of reach. It's called child-proofing. Some parents rationalize their refusal to child-proof by saying, "He's got to learn what he can and cannot touch." These are usually the same parents who follow the tyke around all day long, slapping his hands and scolding—a great and counterproductive waste of emotion and effort that does nothing but set the stage for ongoing power struggles.

Keep in mind also that some two-year-olds can be "moved" with spankings while others will only be moved to even greater determination. In the latter case, a vicious cycle can quickly develop: child misbehaves, parent swats; child misbehaves again, parent swats again, harder this time; child misbehaves again, determined to have his way, parent swats several times; child screams and bites parent, parent unloads on child. In the process, nothing is accomplished. This age child also tends to quickly forget consequences. Even if a spanking stops a toddler from doing something, the likelihood is he'll be back doing the same thing within five minutes or less. He's not necessarily being rebellious; he's simply acting his age.

When all is said and done, whether or not spankings will "work" with this age child is something that can be answered only through experiment. In any case, the same rules apply: spank as a first resort, with your open hand, on the child's rear end only, and having terminated the misbehavior (if, in fact, it terminates) and secured the child's attention, deliver a short reprimand. Following up with the modified time-out technique described above may also be helpful. For a more thorough discussion of how to discipline toddlers, I refer the reader to *Making the "Terrible" Twos Terrific!*, by yours truly (Andrews and McMeel, 1993).

Q. How young is too young for a spanking?

A. In order for spankings to be effective, a child must be capable of understanding what it is the parents are trying to communicate with the spanking and the reprimand that follows. This means that spankings are pointless with children younger than eighteen months, at the very least. As a general rule, I do not recommend popping the "heinies" of children younger than two. The other factor that comes into play with infants and young toddlers is the heightened risk of physical injury, however unintentional. The force of the swat needs to be modified accordingly.

Q. Our thirty-month-old daughter, when we pop her behind to get her attention, always says, in a scolding tone, "Stop that!" It's as if the tables have suddenly turned, and we're the ones in the wrong. How should we respond to her?

A. I've heard the same story from many parents of toddlers. The best way to respond to the child's indignance is to simply say, "Yes, that's right, I want you to stop that." Immediately, direct the child to another activity or item, as in, "Go play with your blocks or your teddy bear." Remember that with all children, but with this age child especially, in hesitation all is lost.

Q. After a child receives a spanking, should the parent immediately reassure the child that he's still loved?

A. If parents follow my guidelines for spanking, there should be no need for reassurances. In fact, because any reassurances might be interpreted as an apology of sorts, they might well neutralize the message the parent was sending the child via his or her rear end. My sense is that parents who feel compelled to reassure their children after spankings usually do so more to ease their guilt than to ease their children's supposed fears of no longer being loved. If a parent spanks properly, and the child feels loved to begin with, there's little if any chance the child will suddenly feel rejected. If parents spank quickly and without hurtful intent, but simply to move the child rapidly back onto the right track, they have no reason to feel guilty and the child has no reason to feel wronged.

Aside from that general rule, however, if a child comes

to a parent after a spanking and asks to be held or loved in some way, then the parent has an obligation to comfort, understanding that this is probably the child's way of offering an apology for his misdeed. Do not, however, apologize for having spanked the child, as this will give the child permission to test limits again.

Q. **After one of my mild spankings, my five-year-old will sit and sulk or sob to get my attention. If I ignore her, she will go on and on for as long as forty-five minutes (which is as long as I've been able to stand it). What should I do?**

A. Under no circumstances should a child be allowed to put on a prolonged dramatic display of victimhood after a spanking. When your daughter does so, send her to her room with instructions to sulk and sob all she wants there and there only. Our daughter, Amy, was equally inclined to make a theatrical production out of a spanking. First, she would howl as if mortally wounded, then she'd mope around dejectedly, obviously wanting the spotlight. (Amy went on to a brilliant, if brief, career in community theater.) On these occasions, we simply banished her to her room for a minimum of thirty minutes or as long as it took for her to regain her composure. As soon as we directed her to her cubicle, she would straighten up and say, "I'm okay! I'll stop!" Without question, she knew exactly what she was doing and was in complete control of her psychological state. Consistent with our no-warnings policy when it came to discipline, we'd respond, "Yes, Amy, you're okay, and you can take all the time you need to stop in your room. Now, go! We'll let you know when thirty minutes is up." (By the way, the rule in the Rosemond household was that if the child in question asked if the time was up yet, the time started over.) Thirty minutes was all it ever took for Amy to return to us from her sojourn to Hollywood.

Q. My four-year-old, after I spank him, which isn't that often, tells me in a rather sassy tone of voice that it didn't hurt. I don't know how I should respond to this, if at all. Any ideas?

A. Remember that a "Rosemond-style" spanking isn't designed to be physically painful, only shocking. So, the next time your son tells you that a spanking didn't hurt, say, "Oh, that's good. I wasn't trying to hurt you. I was just trying to get your attention, and it obviously worked." Then, follow through with a consequence of one sort or another, as discussed earlier in this chapter.

Q. Should children be spanked on their bare bottoms, or does it matter?

A. Yes, it matters, and no, children should not be spanked on their bare bottoms unless their bottoms are bare to begin with. In other words, if a child misbehaves in some flagrant way while undressed, as in getting ready for a bath or bed, then a swat to the bare bottom is fine. But children should not suffer the humiliation of having to take clothes off or pull them down in order to expose their bottoms. I can't say it enough: The purpose is not to cause pain (although a transient sting is probably unavoidable and not at all undesirable). The old "you're not going to be able to sit down for a week!" spanking is definitely not a '90s thing.

Q. Do you approve of spanking a thirteen-year-old for not minding?

A. As a general rule, I don't approve of spanking children who have reached either puberty or adolescence, which-ever comes first. In fact, I feel that spankings are generally ineffective past age nine or ten. If by this age you've been successful at commanding the child's respect, then spank-ings should be completely unnecessary. If you haven't, then all the spankings in the world won't help you paddle back upstream. This is not to say that if your discipline hasn't been effective by age nine or ten, it's too late, but rather that the disciplinary overhaul is going to require a concerted, sustained, and highly systematic effort, one that spankings won't enhance. In that case, some of the suggestions for disciplinary follow-through described earlier in this chapter might prove helpful.

Now, having said all that, I must admit to having popped my son's behind on one occasion when he was thirteen. I was explaining, or attempting to explain, why I would not allow him to go somewhere with a group of his friends. Not trying to reason with him, mind you, but simply trying to give him my reasons. He was highly agitated and was interrupting me every few seconds. Finally, I swatted his behind so quickly he didn't even see it coming. One time.

"Hey!" he yelled.

"Hey," I answered. "Are you ready to listen, or do you need to run off at the mouth some more? If you do, then the price you pay will be spending the remainder of the day in your room. What'll it be?"

"Uh, I guess I'll listen," he answered, a slight pout at the corners of his mouth.

"Good choice!" I said, and proceeded, uninterrupted, with my explanation. When I was done, he said he thought my reasons would be understandable if he were younger, but were clearly inappropriate for a man of the world such as himself.

"Oh, Eric," I said, "if I was your age, I wouldn't agree with me, either. I wasn't asking you to agree, nor did I expect you to agree. I only expect you to obey, and I trust that you will." With that, I walked away, leaving him to— as my stepfather used to put it—"stew in his own juices."

So you see, I broke my own edict concerning spanking teenagers. I offer no defense except to say the spank to Eric's thirteen-year-old behind was a one-time exception to the rule. Furthermore, I have no regrets. Given the same

circumstances, I'd do it again, which only goes to show that to everything, there is a season.

Q. You've said that teachers shouldn't spank students, but what about grandparents or stepparents?

A. That's a tough one, the answer depending on just how close a relationship the child in question enjoys with the grandparents or stepparent. I have to say that in this day and age, most grandparents don't qualify as spankers by virtue of not being able to spend a lot of time with their grandchildren. Just because grandparents love their grandchildren and their grandchildren love them isn't enough. They must be spending lots of time together on an ongoing basis in order for spankings to work. If the grandparents live in the home or are a daily presence in the child's life, and they enjoy an excellent relationship with the child, then a spanking every now and then is not going to be disruptive. But even if the above conditions are met, grandparents should not spank unless the parents have given them permission to do so, and unless they are willing to do so according to the same guidelines.

A stepparent qualifies as a spanker if (1) the child lives in the home, and (2) the stepparent and the child enjoy an extremely affectionate relationship, one that is marked by a lot of respect on the part of the child. My stepfather, who's spankings I described in chapter 2, did not qualify as a spanker because he wasn't warm and approachable. Nonetheless, he spanked. As a result of the fact that I had little respect for him to begin with, his spankings only caused me to resent him further. Looking back, I have to believe he sensed my resentment, which only drove him to become that much more frustrated with me and become that much more inclined to spank. The vicious cycle that developed is almost inevitable under the circumstances. Did his spankings qualify as child abuse? I think so, especially those which were air-mailed via belt. Nonetheless, I don't feel emotionally scarred from the experience, which might not be the case had the belt behind the spankings been my Dad's, as opposed to someone's with whom I had the choice of emotional attachment. In fact, although there's no way of justifying his actions toward me as a child, I forgive my stepfather for what he did and didn't do. He was an emotionally limited individual who, although highly intelligent, truly didn't know any better.

Q. Is it ever appropriate for a parent to spank in a public situation, such as in a store, or at a family gathering?

A. No! Public spankings are humiliating to a child, and the self-conscious feelings that ensue are likely to drive further misbehavior. Furthermore, in a public situation the child is too aware of the presence of other people to focus sufficiently on the parent and, therefore, the message. Lastly, publicly administered spankings are downright inconsiderate of other people, who have no desire whatsoever to watch other parents spank their kids. If a child begins to misbehave in a public setting, and the parent feels that a spanking is warranted to set the child back on track, the parent should remove the child to a private area before applying open hand to derriere.

Q. If being spanked in public is humiliating to a child, then aren't you saying it's emotionally abusive to spank a child in, say, a shopping center?

A. No, that's not what I'm saying. Abuse isn't a matter of some fleeting effect—in this case, humiliation—a child experiences in response to a parent's disciplinary actions. It's a matter of *lasting* effect. I'm saying that the humiliation and the presence of other people make it difficult for the child to focus on the parent and the message. Therefore, public spankings are ineffective. I also say that they create discomfort on the part of people present, who have no choice in the matter. In short, a public spanking is *rude*. If I had my way, parents who spanked in public would be cited not for child abuse, but for disturbing the public peace.

Q. Should I ever spank my child for something he did when he was with some other adult, like at a friend's house?

A. My spanking guidelines, as set forth in chapter 2, answer the question. If a spanking is only useful to terminate an objectionable behavior, secure the child's attention, express disapproval, and remind the child of your authority, then spanking for something a child did while with another adult seems relatively pointless. After all, the behavior in question is already a thing of the past.

The question then becomes, Should you punish your child for a misbehavior that occurred in the presence of another adult? The answer is yes, but a reprimand might be sufficient. In any case, you have a responsibility to respond to the child's extrafamilial transgression in some demonstrative way.

Let's say you decide to simply reprimand and let it go at that, and your child begins to defend himself or refuses to accept responsibility for his actions. In that case, a swift swat telegraphed to his behind might serve to terminate his jabber and rivet his attention upon your message.

Q. If my child misbehaves with me during the day, is it appropriate for me to tell his father when he gets home, and for his father to then spank? What if I've already spanked?

A. I'll take your questions one at a time. First, if your child misbehaves at home during the day, it is entirely appropriate for you to inform your husband when he gets home. In fact, in most cases it would be inappropriate for you *not* to inform your husband, the exceptions involving minor, garden-variety infractions that are the inevitable by-products of immaturity. Second, whether you spanked or not, I don't think it's generally appropriate for your husband to do so when he comes home (see my answer to the question immediately preceding this one). It's entirely appropriate, however, for you to delay deciding how to punish your child until your husband gets home, as long as it's clear that you're not doing so to make your husband the heavy, but to demonstrate your solidarity as a couple. In that sense, I happen to believe in waiting "until your father gets home."

Q. My four-year-old laughs at me when I spank him. I've tried spanking him harder, but that doesn't work. What would you recommend?

A. The way you phrase your questions implies that you are using spankings as punishment for misbehavior. As I've already said, spankings are not an effective form of punishment. In and of themselves, they are inconsequential. The punishment, if one seems appropriate, should *follow* the spanking.

Your child laughs at you when you spank because despite his tender years he realizes that your spankings are "fruitless." If when he misbehaves all he suffers is a relatively minor, fleeting sting on his rear end, so what? That's more than worth seeing Mom get flustered. And better yet, he can get you even more flustered if he laughs!

I have to agree with your son. As it stands (assuming I read you correctly), your spankings are a joke, and the bigger the punch line (aren't I clever?), the more he's bound to laugh. If you want your son to take your spankings seriously, then follow the guidelines set forth in chapter 2. Don't get mean. Mean business!

Q. If children aren't made violent by spankings, then how is it that some children become highly aggressive, while others don't?

A. Spankings do not a violent person make, but if a child is regularly beaten by parents who are rejecting, there is a greater-than-good chance the child will become either depressed or easily frustrated and reflexively aggressive—verbally, physically, or both. One or the other end result is also likely in the case of a child who grows up with adults who engage in regular bouts of verbal and/or physical violence. But it has never been shown that the inclination to "pass it on" is a consequence of spankings which are prudently administered. It is my personal and professional experience that children who are spanked by loving parents usually act appreciative of the fact their parents "brought them back to earth." My wife and I often remarked, concerning both of our children, that a spanking not only accomplished the immediate goal—stopping the misbehavior and securing the child's attention—but also resulted in a rather sweeping, and relatively long-lasting, "altitude adjustment." A couple of well-placed swats to the rear often turned a child who'd been increasingly difficult to live with into a communicative, affectionate being who was actually a joy to be around. As Dr. James Dobson, writing in *The New Dare to Discipline* (1992), points out, "A boy or girl who knows love abounds at home will not resent a well-deserved spanking. One who is unloved or ignored will hate *any* form of discipline." Truer words have never been spoken, as attested to by my boyhood experience with my stepfather.

Q. **Please tell us what concerned citizens can do to combat the possibility of antispanking legislation that—with the political correctness that's infecting America—may be coming sooner than we'd like.**

A. Get in touch, and *stay in touch,* with the state and national legislators that represent your district. Ask them if antispanking legislation of any sort—including legislation that could eventually produce antispanking laws, as in a Children's Rights Amendment—has been proposed and, if so, by whom. Let your representatives know—*in writing*— what your feelings are on this subject. If they are already opposed to laws of this sort, ask if there's anything you can do at a grass-roots level to help defeat such legislation. Inform other parents about the possibility of and dangers inherent to such laws and encourage them to write their representatives as well. If a legislator is planning to sponsor such a law, call his office and see if you can discover what special-interest group has lobbied him for this cause. (Keep in mind that the idea did not, in all likelihood, originate with the legislator.) Find out who sits on that organization's board of directors and write these folks letters asking them to consider the threat to individual liberties and the autonomy of the American family posed by such laws. Be sure and write the sponsoring legislator a well-thought-out letter stating your opposition to this idea. If enough people write such letters, perhaps he'll reconsider his position. Better yet, send him a copy of this book.

AFTERWORD

by S. DuBose Ravenel, M.D., F.A.A.P.

John Rosemond has identified and written about an important subject—disciplinary spanking—that is currently the focus of heated debate in America. John has challenged us to look beyond the politically correct view that spanking is inherently inappropriate, if not abusive—a view that has dominated professional writing in medical and psychological journals for more than a decade. My experiences as (1) a child who was the recipient of occasional spankings, (2) a father who administered occasional spankings, (3) a pediatrician who has worked with parents for more than a deĉade, and (4) a faculty member in the pediatric department of a major university medical school, affirm John's very sensible conclusions and recommendations.

As the childhood recipient of occasional well-deserved spankings by my father, it never occurred to me, nor has it since, that appropriately administered physical discipline teaches that violence is acceptable or instills a violent bent in the personality as many self-proclaimed antispanking "experts" would have us believe. Nor do the overwhelming majority of my peers display violent tendencies, de3spite the fact that almost all children of my generation were spanked by their parents.

My two children, now twenty-one and twenty-three years of age, can also recall occasional spankings. They do not and have never believed that the antispanking myths are true. As a matter of fact, they tell me that when the time comes, they intend to raise their own children pretty much the same way they were raised. I think it's fair to say that neither of them is a psychological or social misfit.

Not only does the anecdotal evidence fail to support the

claims made by antispanking zealots, but the best scientific data fail to support them as well. In 1973, researcher Diana Baumrind discovered that authoritative parenting was associated with more maturity in children than either authoritarian or permissive parenting styles. Baumrind also found that authoritative parents were apt to occasionally spank their kids. Most interesting, permissive parents, who generally refrained from expressing anger toward their children, were found to be even more prone than authoritarian parents to sudden, explosive parental rages. This suggests that parent-child conflicts are less likely to escalate to the flash point when parents feel free to curtail such escalations by spanking.

During my eleven years of service as a member of the pediatric faculty in a residency training program (1976 to 1987), the striking contrast between what I believed concerning spanking and the prevailing view held by those who addressed the subject in academic publications became increasingly evident. This prompted me to seek out and review all of the available evidence. I came to the conclusion that there was little, if any, substance to the notion that spanking was abusive or even counterproductive. The evidence was lacking, but the bias characteristic of many of the researchers was plain to see. Rather than practicing disciplined science, they were promoting a child-rearing ideology. No one, however, seemed willing to say that the emperor had no clothes. As a result, the often irresponsible rhetoric of antispanking proponents continues unabated today, even in the medical profession. Recent examples of this include:

• The March 1982 *Newsletter of the Section on Child Abuse and Neglect of the American Academy of Pediatrics* contained a commentary on corporal punishment in the home in which pediatricians were appropriately encouraged to recommend alternative methods of discipline. Rather than advocate that pediatricians also teach appropriate uses of spanking, the commentary contained statements that blurred the distinction between spanking and abuse. For example, corporal punishment was defined as "any action that produces physical discomfort, such as spanking, shaking, pinching, ear pulling, jabbing, shoving, choking, denying bathroom privileges, withholding water or food." Any reasonable person would immediately recognize that spanking and choking do not belong in the same category. Nor do spanking and shaking, pinching, ear pulling, etc. The authors went on to say, "Spanking may contribute to delinquency and counterproductive behavior." In the case of a child being struck abusively, and frequently so, that may be true. However, as Baumrind's research attests, occasional appropriately administered spankings may well *prevent* delinquency and other antisocial behaviors. It could be argued, furthermore, that *any* parenting behavior, in the extreme, may lead to aberrant behavior in a child. For example, it is possible that overprotection and "smothering" may contribute, in some cases, to irresponsible, antisocial behaviors. Nonetheless, no one would suggest that loving a child places the child at risk.

• In *Caring for Our Children,* published in 1992 by the American Public Health Association and the American Academy of Pediatrics, we see a further example of the biases and distortions characteristic of antispanking rhetoric. Under "Standards for Child Care" in *all* child-care settings and by *all* caregivers, prohibited behaviors include "corporal punishment, including hitting, spanking, beating, shaking, pinching, and other measures that produce physical pain." Once again, spanking is lumped together with obviously abusive forms of behavior as though they were one and the same.

Although the above statements do not represent the official position of the American Academy of Pediatrics (AAP), they do represent that of an important committee within the academy. It appears, however, that statements of that sort do not reflect the views of the majority of AAP members. In a 1992 survey of Ohio pediatricians and fam-

ily physicians, 59 percent of the 197 pediatricians partici-
pating in the survey expressed support for the use of corporal punishment, defined (and appropriately so) as striking the child's buttocks or hand with the hand. In a similar
survey of 130 pediatricians in 1993, two-thirds expressed
similar support for parental spanking.

Recently a systematic review of the literature was done
and presented at the 1993 Annual Meeting of the Section
on Bio-Ethics of the AAP. The researchers reviewed every
article (132 in all) published over a ten-year period (1984–
1993) in psychological, sociological, and other clinical research journals in which corporal punishment or spanking
was addressed. Only *one* of these articles contained any
useful data as well as a reasonable definition of corporal
punishment, and this one study *failed to document any un-
toward consequences of disciplinary spanking.* In short, Rosemond's assertion that the claims of the antispanking movement are based on rhetoric rather than scientific evidence
appears to be right on the money.

I commend John Rosemond for affirming what most parents already know, in their hearts, to be true: spankings,
used conservatively and properly by a loving parent, can be
not only an effective disciplinary adjunct, but can also help
create respect for parents early in life, thus contributing to
respect for self and others later in life. John has moved the
debate over spanking to a new, refreshing level of objectivity
and common sense. He has exposed the antispanking movement for what it is—an ideological agenda intended to re-
verse the wisdom of generations of parents, the teaching of
the Scriptures, and research supporting the appropriate-
ness of properly administered disciplinary spanking.

*S. DuBose Ravenel, M.D., F.A.A.P., practices
medicine out of the High Point Infant and Child
Clinic, High Point, North Carolina. He is a former
Clinical Associate Professor of Pediatrics (1976–87) at
the University of North Carolina School of Medicine.*

HIGHLY RECOMMENDED READING

Dobson, James. *The New Dare to Discipline.* Wheaton, Ill.: Tyndale House Publishers, 1992.

————. *Parenting Isn't for Cowards.* Waco, Tex.: Word Books, 1987.

Mason, Mary Ann, and Eileen Gambill, eds. *Debating Children's Lives: Current Controversies on Children and Adolescents.* Thousand Oaks, Calif.: Sage Publications, 1994.

Rosemond, John. *John Rosemond's Six-Point Plan for Raising Happy, Healthy Children.* Kansas City, Mo.: Andrews and McMeel, 1989.

————. *Making the "Terrible" Twos Terrific!* Kansas City, Mo.: Andrews and McMeel, 1993.

————. *Parent Power: A Common Sense Approach to Parenting in the '90s and Beyond.* Kansas City, Mo.: Andrews and McMeel, 1991.

Wexler, Richard. *Wounded Innocents: The Real Victims of the War Against Child Abuse.* Buffalo, N.Y.: Prometheus Books, 1990.

BIBLIOGRAPHY

Bradshaw, John. "Never Knowing Who We Are: A traditional upbringing teaches that we're more lovable when we're not ourselves." *Lears,* January 1993: 42.

Briggs, Dorothy. *Your Child's Self-Esteem.* New York: Doubleday & Co., 1970.

Dobson, James. *The New Dare to Discipline.* Wheaton, Ill.: Tyndale House Publishers, 1992.

Dubin, Murray. "To Spank or to Spare." *Philadelphia Inquirer,* October 1, 1993.

EPOCH-Worldwide. *Hitting People Is Wrong—and Children Are People Too.* London: Association for the Protection of All Children, 1992.

Fraiberg, Selma. *The Magic Years.* New York: Charles Scribner's Sons, 1959.

Gill, Charles D. "Essay on the Status of the American Child, 2000 A.D.: Chattel or Constitutionally Protected Child-Citizen?" *Ohio Northern University Law Review,* vol. 17, no. 3 (1991): 543–79.

Gordon, Thomas. *Parent Effectiveness Training.* New York: Peter H. Wyden, Inc., 1970.

Larzelere, Robert E. "Response to Oosterhuis: Empirically Justified Uses of Spanking: Toward a Discriminating View of Corporal Punishment." *Journal of Psychology and Theology,* 1993, vol. 21, no. 2: 142–147.

———. "Should Use of Corporal Punishment by Parents be Considered Abusive?—No." In *Debating Children's Lives,* Mary Ann Mason and Eileen Gambrill, eds. Newbury Park, Calif.: Sage Publications, 1994.

Marvel Comics, in cooperation with the National Committee for Prevention of Child Abuse. *The Amazing Spider-Man and the New Mutants,* vol. 1, no. 1, 1990.

National Committee for Prevention of Child Abuse, Board

of Directors. *Position Statement on Physical Punishment.* Adopted May 1989, Chicago.

———. *How to Teach Your Children Discipline.* Chicago: National Committee for Prevention of Child Abuse, 1990.

New American Standard Bible. New York: Thomas Nelson Publishers, 1979.

Rosemond, John. *Making the "Terrible" Twos Terrific!* Kansas City, Mo.: Andrews and McMeel, 1993.

———. "Should Use of Corporal Punishment by Parents be Considered Abusive?—No." In *Debating Children's Lives,* Mary Ann Mason and Eileen Gambrill, eds. Newbury Park, Calif.: Sage Publications, 1994.

Spock, Benjamin M. *Baby and Child Care.* Revised edition. New York: Pocket Books, 1968.

Straus, Murray. "Should Use of Corporal Punishment by Parents be Considered Abusive?—Yes." In *Debating Children's Lives,* Mary Ann Mason and Eileen Gambrill, eds. Newbury Park, Calif.: Sage Publications, 1994.

Wexler, Richard. Letter to John Rosemond, December 7, 1993.

———. *Wounded Innocents—The Real Victims of the War Against Child Abuse.* Buffalo, N.Y.: Prometheus Books, 1990.

ABOUT THE AUTHOR

Family psychologist, author, and speaker John Rosemond is director of the Center for Affirmative Parenting (CAP), headquartered in Gastonia, North Carolina. CAP is a national parent resource center whose primary activity is to provide workshops and other educational presentations for parents and professionals who work with children and families. CAP also provides a variety of print, audio, and video materials on parenting, child development, and family values.

Since 1978, John has written a nationally syndicated parenting column which currently appears in 125 newspapers across the United States, including the Pacific edition of *Stars and Stripes,* the newspaper of the U.S. Armed Services. John is also the featured parenting columnist for both *Better Homes and Gardens* and *Hemispheres,* United Air Lines' in-flight magazine.

To Spank or Not to Spank is John's fifth book for Andrews and McMeel. His first, *John Rosemond's Six-Point Plan for Raising Happy, Healthy Children* (1989), which *Esquire* magazine called "refreshingly reactionary," became a best-seller in 1990 and continues to be one of the most popular parenting books of the '90s. *Ending the Homework Hassle* (1990), *Parent Power!* (1991), and *Making the "Terrible" Twos Terrific!* (1993) followed to equally good sales and reviews.

In 1981, John was selected "Professional of the Year" by the Mecklenburg County Mental Health Association of Charlotte, North Carolina. In 1986, he was presented with the Alumni Achievement Award by his alma mater, Western Illinois University.

In addition to his other accomplishments, John is one of America's busiest and most popular public speakers. In

1993 alone, John made 225 presentations in 175 sites across the United States. His parenting presentations and workshops draw consistently rave reviews from parents and professionals alike.

Last, but by no means least, John is husband of twenty-six-plus years to Willie, and father to Eric—twenty-five, married, and a commercial pilot—and Amy—twenty-two and a senior at the University of North Carolina. John and Willie are anticipating the birth of their first grandchild in December 1994.

Anyone interested in obtaining further information concerning John or CAP may do so by writing The Center for Affirmative Parenting, P.O. Box 4124, Gastonia, North Carolina 28054, or calling (704) 864-1012.

ABOUT THE ILLUSTRATOR

Jeff Koterba is an editorial cartoonist for the *Omaha World-Herald*, Nebraska's largest daily. He is also father to Josh, eight, who has more than once provided inspiration for Jeff's work.

Rumor has it that when he finds the time, Jeff picks a pretty mean mandolin, too.